ePrabhavnomics

PRABHAV MEHARUNKAR

DEDICATION

This book is dedicated to anyone who is interested in studying economics in further education years. But everyone is free to read this book, and no preliminary knowledge is required to understand this book.

ACKNOWLEDGMENTS

I would like to thank everyone who has helped me through this journey of 100 blogs. My family, my relatives, my friends, my schoolteachers who have always encouraged and supported my blogs and shared their opinion on them. I would also like to credit the websites I used for my research.

ePrabhavnomics blog 1

Originally Published on: 9 September 2018

What if 1 dollar = 1 rupee?

Have you ever wondered what would happen if 1 dollar was equal to 1 rupee? Well it is highly unlikely for this to happen, but just imagine, how will our lives be different if overnight 1 dollar was equal to 1 rupee? So in this blog I will tell you what will happen, if 1 dollar was equal to 1 rupee.

Before beginning I wanted to clarify one misconception, a stronger currency doesn't mean a bigger economy.

For example 1 Bangladeshi taka= 1.32 Japanese yen. And I don't think I have to tell which country has a bigger economy

Importing goods in India will be cheaper. For example if a US good costs $2M, importing it to India ($1= Indian rupees 68) would have cost Indian rupees 136M. Now import will cost only Indian rupees 2M.

Due to cheaper imports, people can buy more luxurious goods, as they will become cheaper. Petrol prices will also go down, thus leading to less transport cost across the country.

Now you might be wondering, this all looks good. But remember there are two sides to every coin. Meaning if there are good effects then there are also some bad effects to 1 dollar equalling 1 rupee.

Exporting goods from India will be dearer.

For example if an Indian export to US costs Indian rupees 68M, it would cost $1M to US ($1= Indian rupees 68). Now it will cost $68M to US.

People will lose their jobs, as labour cost in India will increase.

For example if a company pays Indian rupees 68K ($1K) to their workers, ($1=Indian rupees 68). After the change in exchange rate ($1=Indian rupees 1) the labour cost in India will go up ($68K in India) ($1K in US), therefore the company will prefer to pay someone $1K rather $68K.

This way the IT and service sector will be gone, and companies will start to move out.

No countries will invest in India due to higher export cost. But will instead invest in countries where it is cheaper.

ePrabhavnomics blog 2

Originally Published on: 16 September 2018

Why is the US dollar such a strong currency?

Have you ever wondered why the US dollar is such a strong currency? Well, today I am going to answer this question.

A country with high debt could see a fall in the strength of its currency, when the investors fear that the country can go in debt default (a failure to pay interest or loan on principal or security when due), and in fear they start selling government bonds of that country. In case of US investors are fairly confident that the country won't go in debt default. And investors prefer to invest or hold bonds instead of invest in the EU (currently not politically stable).

The US took these steps to keep investors' confidence high.

Higher interest rates of US bonds relative to other countries. Every country issues their bonds with foreign investors, US has issued a bond of 1.80% to foreign investors, this is higher than the interest rates bond other countries. Due to higher interest rate bonds, many foreigners have been attracted to the US dollar.

The US has improved its trade balance (calculated exports minus imports). A improvement in the trade balance means imports to the US have decreased, meanwhile exports from the US have increased. This has caused more US dollars to remain in the US. It has also helped in increasing US energy production.

The US has taken many measures to reduce budget deficit. In some cases harsh ones, such as reduce spending, and increasing taxes. For example in 2010 US had a 11% of GDP budget deficit, this reduced to 3% by end of 2014.

The euro saw a decrease in value against the dollar over the past few years, this meant the dollar automatically got stronger in value. This is because the euro makes up 57.6% of the value of US dollar index (an index used to measure the value of the US dollar relative to a basket of foreign currencies). Therefore whatever makes the euro weaker makes the dollar stronger.

To conclude the US dollar has a debt of $18 trillion, its currency remains strong due to high investment in the country.

ePrabhavnomics blog 3

Originally Published on: 23 September 2018

Why is the Euro stronger than the US dollar?

The current Euro-US Dollar exchange rate is US\$1.18=€1. This means the Euro is stronger than the US dollar, have you ever wondered why? Well, today I will be explaining why the Euro is stronger.

First factor that we will look at is Supply and Demand for the currencies. The value of a currency is usually dictated by the supply and demand for that currency. Demand for a currency goes up by economic growth and by investor interest (an amount of interest that is paid on loan proceeds to purchase investments or securities). Supply is regulated by monetary policies (a policy laid by central banks to manage money supply and interest rates). The Federal Reserve increase the supply of dollars, in response to a deflationary (something that deflates economy) crisis, this therefore lowered the value of the dollar.

The next factor is Interest Rates. One of the reasons why the dollar is weaker than the euro is because of their relative interest rates. During economic contraction (phase when economy growth is negative) the US reacted quickly by cutting interest rates. The European Central Bank (ECB) waited for few month before starting to cut interest rates, but they never took the rates as low as the Federal Reserve did. In US the interest rates were lowered to about zero, meanwhile the ECB stopped at an interest rate of 1%. A higher interest rate means, the currency increases in value, this meant the Euro increased in value, while the Dollar decreased in value.

Another major reason why the dollar fell against the euro was quantitative easing (introduction of new money into the money supply by a Central Bank). This refers to a monetary policy strategy in which the central bank reduces its quality standards, and accepts for loans to increase volume of lending. The Federal Reserve has participated in quantitative easing to stimulate domestic economy, while ECB has restricted such measures.

The 21st century saw a major global trend towards diversification of currency reserves, this had an inevitable effect on weakening the dollar. Large holder of foreign currency reserves, mainly China, thought it was their best interest to diversify their holdings into euros and other currencies rather than primarily dollars. Major oil-supplying countries have also expressed a desire to put oil prices in euros and local currencies instead of dollars. This reduces demand for dollars, thus favouring euro over dollar.

ePrabhavnomics blog 4

Originally Published on: 30 September 2018

What if only one currency was used around the world?

Dollars, Euros, Rupees. Why do we have so many currencies? Why can't we all just share the same currency? Have you ever had this question in mind? If yes, you are not alone, even I have had this question in mind. So today I will be answering this question.

A single currency around the world will help improve communication, and there will be a price transparency (ability to know all of the bid prices, ask prices and trading quantities for a given stock, good or service at any point in time) when importing and exporting goods.

The cost of doing business internationally will reduce, meaning that competitive companies will go and do business in every country possible. This will lead to many 'Multi National Corporations' and will increase the competition in the market, which is good for the general public.

A single currency will eliminate risk of currency crisis and hyperinflation.

Developing countries will benefit hugely if the whole world had the same currency, this is because they can get a lot of business trust (a form of business organisation, in which investors receive transferable certificates of beneficial interest). Thus forming a base for the country's future economic development.

If every country had the same currency, 'exchange rates' wouldn't exist. This will eliminate uncertainty of exchange rates, and interest rates and inflation will be low.

Sounds good? Well, every situation has pros and cons, and this isn't an exception. There are also many cons to having a single currency.

Due to there being no exchange rates investors can easily shift their investment, when a country is facing some temporary problems. Therefore due to these rapid investment fluctuations it can badly affect a country's growth.

It will be harder for the Central Bank to make decisions, this is because every country has a different economic structure and status. And a single currency will mean developed nations and developing nations come in the same basket. So the Central Bank will find it difficult to make decisions (such as interest rates) that will benefit every country.

A single currency can increase black money from time to time, because money can easily be shifted from one country to another and go unnoticed. This can damage the economies of developing countries.

The economic collapse of a country can spread to other countries and lead to a global financial crisis, causing a great depression.

Lastly, some countries may take pride in using their own currency rather than sharing the same currency with other countries.

Overall the disadvantages outweigh the advantages, meaning that in the present scenarios a single currency is impractical. And a brief answer to why 'different currencies have different values': higher the demand for one currency, higher its value. Higher demand for a currency is due to a country producing more needed goods or quality goods.

ePrabhavnomics blog 5

Originally Published on: 7 October 2018

How to measure the economic development of a country?

Ever wondered how developed your country is? How does the development of your country compare to that of other countries? Well, there are many factors that influence how developed a country is. In this blog I will explain all these factors and what they show, and after I will give some data to show which countries are at the top and at the bottom in each one of these factor.

So the first factor we will look at is 'life expectancy'. Life expectancy shows the average number of years that a person can expect to live to, based on their birth year. This is a useful factor to measure economic development of a country, because it shows how good the health sector of that country is, a country with a higher life expectancy has a better health care, so is better off. As of today, the country with highest life expectancy is Japan with 85.30 years, and the lowest is Chad with 50.60 years.

The next factor we will be looking at is 'infant mortality rate', (IMR). IMR shows the number of infants that die before reaching their 1st birthday, given there are 1,000 births in a year (meaning that if there were only 1,000 births in a year, how many infant would die out of those 1,000). This factor tells us how good the health sector of the country is and also how educated/old the mother is. Because an older mother is usually more educated than a younger mother, so a later first birth usually reduces chances of infant deaths, this time the country with a lower score has the upper-hand. Japan again is the best with only 2/1000 infant deaths, meanwhile Afghanistan has the worst score with 110.60/1000.

This will be the first factor not relating to health, which we will be looking at 'GDP per capita'. GDP is Gross Domestic Product, which is the total number of goods and services produced by a country in a year. GDP per capita is the total GDP of the country divided by the population of that country (total GDP ÷ total population), just for simplicity to compare, every country's GDP per capita is shown in US dollars ($). This shows on average how wealthy the people in the country are. Here the country with a higher rank is wealthier. Qatar takes the lead this time with a GDP per capita of $124,500, meanwhile Burundi is at the bottom with only $700.

Literacy Rate tells us, the percentage of the population above 15 years of age that are able to read and write, a simple sentence. This factor tells us how good the education sector of the country is. The higher the literacy rate the more developed the country. North Korea tops here with a 100% literacy rate, while Niger is at the bottom with only 19.1% literacy.

Education Index is another factor showing how good a country's education sector is, with it containing two sub-factors which are merged to make a final score. The education index score is between 0 and 1, with 1 being the highest/best meanwhile 0 being the lowest/worst.

The first sub-factor is 'mean years of schooling' it shows the average number of years of education received by people aged 25 and older in their lifetime. Again a higher score shows that a country has the upper-hand, with Switzerland topping with 13.4 years and Burkina Faso at the bottom with only 1.4 years.

The second sub-factor is 'expected years of schooling' it shows the average number of years a child is expected to attend school or university. And the topper here is Australia with 20.4 years, while South Sudan is at the other end of the rank with only 4.9 years expected os schooling.

Overall, on the education index Australia tops again with a score of 0.939 and Niger having the lowest of 0.206.

Human Development Index (HDI) is the last factor that we will be looking at. HDI is a score given to every country from 1 highest/best and 0 lowest/worst, and having with 4 economic development factors being merged into it (life expectancy, GDP per capita and education index). Countries according to their HDI are divided into 4 groups; very high human development (score above 0.800), high human development (score between 0.799 and 0.700), medium human development (score between 0.699 and 0.555) and low human development (score below 0.554). Here Norway dominates with 0.953 and Niger scores lowest with 0.354.

These ranks AREN'T made by me, so please DON'T blame me if you feel bad after seeing the ranks.

To see the ranks go to CIA World Factbook, or Wikipedia.

Although a certain country is ranked at the bottom for the moment doesn't mean they can't get to the top of that rank one day.

ePrabhavnomics blog 6
Originally Published on: 14 October 2018

Causes+ Economic impacts of a high young population in a country

Every country has a different age structure (number of people in a certain age group), to be able to compare the age structure of countries, the people are divided into three age groups: young population (age 0-14), working population (ages 15-64) and old population (age 65+).

The population is divided in these three categories, depending on what percentage of the population is part of that category. The middle category (working population) has to look after the other two categories, this is because they (working population) earn income, while the other two don't so they are also called dependent population.

The dependency ratio tells how many dependents a person from the working class has to look after. It is calculated: (young%+old%) ÷ working% x 100. You can also look at the dependency ratio for just one of the two (eg. young% ÷ working% x 100, this is young dependent ratio).

Usually 'more economically developed countries' (MEDCs) have a higher % old population, while 'less economically developed countries' (LEDCs) have a higher % young population. In this blog we will be looking at the causes and economic impacts of a high young population in a country, while the blog of next week will be dedicated to causes and economic Impact of high old population in a country. I will also give an example of a particular country facing the issue which I will speak about in the blog, by looking at various development factors, and some extra factors not necessarily related to development, to understand what each development factor means you will have to read my last blog (blog 5) if you haven't already. I have chosen 'The Gambia' as the country of focus.

The Gambia is an LEDC in Africa ,with an HDI (Human Development Index) of 0.452 which is low. 37.44% of its population is between the ages 0-14, and only 3.48% is above 65. Below are few of its scores in developmental factors, that have caused it to have this population structure, in brackets world average:

Life Expectancy- 65 years (72 years)

Infant Mortality Rate- 60/1000 (29/1000)

Female Literacy Rate- 47.6% (79%)

Expected years of schooling- 9 years (world)

Mother's mean age at first birth (on average how old a woman is when she gives birth to her first child)- 21 years (26 years)

Fertility rate (on average how many children a woman gives birth to in her life)- 3.53 children/woman (2.5)

One of reasons for its high young population is due to, its's poor health care system, which leads to a high infant mortality rate, this forces women to give birth to lots of children so that some children will survive in to adulthood. Poor health care is also the reason of its low life expectancy thus low old population. Most people do not have knowledge of contraception and family planning (caused by low literacy rate). And due very less years of schooling, women start giving birth at an early age, as literacy rate is low many women don't work. Religious beliefs influence families to have more children, and is also considered a status symbol in the society. Due to the country having inadequate pension facilities, when parents get old (45-50 years for them) children will have to look after them and younger children, so more children reduces burden per child.

This has lead to The Gambia's population growth rate being 2.05% annually. (1.09% world average)

The negative economic effects , high young population will lead to include, a strain on education and health care and basic amenities (food, water, etc.). Lack of literacy, due to limited school space in the country, as other young population has taken it up. Infant mortality rate rises due to government unable to get better health care in country. In the future, there will be lots of unemployment (although depends of if job availability increases in future).

There are also some positive economic effects to this, large tax base for the country in future, allowing the government to increase investment. And a possible low dependency ratio in future. The government by managing the situation can help create a more healthy and educated community in the future.

ePrabhavnomics blog 7
Originally Published on: 21 October 2018

Causes+ Economic impacts of a high old population in a country

Last week I wrote a blog on causes and economics impacts in a country that has a high young population. While today's blog will be analysing the opposite problem, which is high old population in a country. Also as you may know from my last blog, 'The Gambia', a 'Less Economically Developed Country' (LEDC) was the example I used, today I will be using the example of a 'More Economically Developed Country' (MEDC) which is 'Japan'.

So as I said in the introduction Japan is an MEDC, and its Human Development Index (HDI) is 0.909 which is very high, Japan is ranked 19th out of 188 countries in the world in terms of HDI. 12.84% of Japan's population is between the ages of 0-14, while 27.84% of its population is above the age of 65. Below are few of its scores on developmental factors, that have caused it to have this population structure, in brackets world average:

Life Expectancy- 85 years (72 years)

Infant Mortality Rate- 2/1000 (29/1000)

Female Literacy Rate- 99% (79%)

Expected Years of Schooling- 15 years (no data available)

Mother's mean age at first birth- 31 years (26 years)

Fertility rate- 1.4 children/woman (2.5)

Japan's high life expectancy (1st in world) is a result of its good health care system. In the 1940s-50s Japan was facing the same problem that The Gambia is facing today (high young population), but due to its good health care, that has significantly improved from then to now, the children from that era have been able to live till their old age. Health care improvements have also helped infant mortality rate to plummet, women can give birth with little fear of their child dying early. Literacy rate of women is high, so they are aware of contraceptive and family planning. Women stay in school for longer and prefer focusing on careers rather than child-bearing. The fertility rate in Japan (1.4) is very low that it is under the replacement fertility rate (the fertility rate a country requires in order to sustain its population) that is 2.1, and due to this Japan's population growth is -0.21%, meaning that Japan's overall population is declining. While the world average population is growing at the rate of 1.09% annually.

The negative economic effects, due to a high old population; there will be a strain on the government into spending more on senior care and pensions, this will be an opportunity cost for the government, as they will have to give up spending on something else (eg. Roads). There will be less youth in the future to support the economy, this will not only increase dependency ratio, but it will leave huge job vacancies. On the other hand if an old person decides not to retire at say 65, his grandchildren who are starting to work, will find it difficult to find a job. People like teachers, who are employed to be with children, will lose their jobs, as less children in the country mean less of them are needed. Meanwhile, most of the workers will only have an opportunity to work in jobs that are for taking care of old. The government in order to not lose its tax revenue will have to raise taxes on workers, as the government has to pay pensions to the old people.

The positive economic effects are, old people can share their experience with their grandchildren. This can prepare the new generation well for the world of work. Manufacturing companies that make products for old people, like Pharma companies (more medicines to old people), will hugely benefit, as they will see a huge increase in their production.

To conclude, both Japan and The Gambia are facing problems due to their respective issues. This way we can say that a country is best off when huge number of its population is in the economically active group, and the other two categories don't have excess population.

ePrabhavnomics blog 8
Originally Published on: 28 October 2018

Why the Indian rupee is falling?

The dollar-rupee conversion rate, as of today, is 1US$= Indian rupees 73.32, and it is expected to go below 75 soon. So, why is this happening? I bet, you are all wondering, and today I will explain this. In my first blog, I wrote about what would happen if the Indian rupee appreciates (goes up) very much that 1 Indian rupees= 1US$, and the impacts weren't so good. But also effects of the Indian rupee depreciating (going down) very much will have negative impacts.

One reason is the extending trade deficit (trade balance calculated: total exports minus total imports, more exports is a trade surplus, while more imports is a trade deficit). According to the data released by the trade ministry of India in July 2018, India recorded a 5-year high trade deficit of $18.02 billion, and it is going up by 8.5% every month. This is mainly due to a 57% annual increase in oil imports. The total imports increased by 28.81% to $43.79 billion, but the exports only increased by 14.32% to $25.77 billion, from last year. The trade deficit is $18.02 billion. A depreciating Indian rupee can help reduce the trade deficit, as Indian exports will seem cheaper to foreign countries, and foreign goods will seem dearer to India.

Although if a foreign good is a necessity in India, the importing of that good may not reduce with higher prices, or exports may not rise if a foreign country doesn't need a particular Indian good. If India's trade deficit doesn't improve, India will have to sell rupees and buy dollars to pay for imports, thus further reducing the value. Higher demand of dollars means its value will go up and reduce value of rupee. You may be wondering what if rupee notes are printed? Its not the solution as it will cause hyperinflation, thus reducing the value of rupee further.

The value of a currency depends on the demand for it, so whenever there is a rise in demand for dollar, it strengthens, this causes the rupee to start losing attraction, so its value goes down. Reasons why the dollar's demand will increase, apart from more tourism in US, the good performance of the US economy, making more people willing to invest in US. Also if a currency tanks overtime like the Turkish Lira, investors will be looking for better currencies, like the dollar, as it gives reasonable returns. So overall, when investors look at US for investment, India loses its charm, and the demand for Indian rupee dips and therefore value also diminishes.

The current trade war that US has started with China, the EU and India, which these countries have reciprocated in the same way. This war has cause the price of imported goods to go up, this will increase the amount of dollars leaving the Indian market. Due to more dollars leaving India and going to US, the demand for the dollar goes up and demand for rupee dips.

Another reason for the rupee's devaluation is the fact that many Indian products aren't used abroad. Mostly US products, like hi-tech equipments, are brought, lots of dollars enter the US, and very few rupees enter India. This leads to less demand for the rupee and this causes a dips in its value.

Did you know, US is the 2nd most visited country in the world, after France, with 75.6 million people visiting the country annually coming from all around the globe? India only experiences 15.5 million tourists annually, means more people demand the dollar over the rupee. US has the highest number of foreign students for university/ higher education, with over 100,000 Indian students going to the US.

Let us look at the Indian side for the impacts the economy will have. India is still not fully sustainably developed, so it has no choice, apart from importing oil, and if the rupee continues depreciating, as I said before, oil prices will rise, and thus increase trade deficit even further. Higher oil prices, means higher transportation cost across the country, and higher prices of consumer goods. Overall, every import will be dearer. As mentioned before, exports could increase with weaker rupee, shortening the trade deficit, but this depends on the necessity of the good to foreign firms.

Overall, the strengthening of the dollar, due to the dollar's increasing demand, is causing a decline in the rupee's value. What India can do in my opinion to help increase demand for the rupee is, improve its tourism (more tourist bring in foreign currency), and strengthen education sector (Indian students will be willing to stay in India, and more foreign students will come for higher education) and creating a niche market for high-tech equipments with such a high youth population. India can't do much for imports and exports, as they both depend of necessity of the good imported/exported. But the question still remains, is the government of India doing anything to manage this situation? Well, you will find out in my next blog.

ePrabhavnomics blog 9

Originally Published on: 4 November 2018

Is the Indian government doing anything to stop the rupee devaluation?

Last week I wrote a blog on why the Indian rupee is constantly devaluating, so today I will be analysing whether the Indian government is doing anything to stop this devaluation. And if they are, why aren't they so successful in stopping this? And what they can do to take control of the situation? The government of India has announced some steps they will take to solve this issue.

The government has taken efforts to reduce unnecessary imports, and to boost more exports. To reduce the unnecessary imports, the government has increased the basic customs duty (a tax that people pay for importing and exporting goods). For example the customs duty for 'Air Conditioners' has increased from 10% to 20%. A higher custom duty will act as a deterrent, for non-essential imports. The customs duty for exports (export tax) is unchanged. Meanwhile to boost exports, the Indian government has set up agri export zones (AEZ). AEZ is a place where farmers can take their final agricultural product, when selling the product to a foreign consumer, from the AEZ the farmer can communicate with the consumer and then the farmers make their product to suit the consumer's demands. India is expected to increase its production of food grain and other agricultural crops, so it has an opportunity to increase agricultural exports. In my opinion India should take advantage of the current US-China trade war, because China has increased import tariff on US goods, so India should study well the products Chinese consumers want. Then Indian producers should focus more on producing products that meet demand of Chinese consumers, and then export these goods to China. This well definitely help reduce trade deficit.

The new 'Make In India' initiative with the view of helping India be the global hub of manufacturing, the Indian government has made manufacturing companies in India able to borrow a maximum of $50M from foreign investors, and giving only 1 year to repay the loan, before the time period off repayment was 3 years. This initiative will help ease foreign borrowing, and fund inflow. Due to this India's foreign debt will decrease, so more people will be willing to invest in India without fear of Indians not repaying the loan.

Masala bonds are bonds denominated in rupees, and are issued in a foreign country for financing medium to long term projects in India. Usually if India borrows money from foreign to finance its projects, India will have to repay this loan to foreign. But conversely with Masala bonds when the foreign investors sign the bond they will have to pay India, in rupees. This increases inflow of rupees in India. A tax exemption will mean foreign investors will have a smaller amount of money to pay to India, this will make Masala bonds more attractive.

An increase in interest rates, this means Indian investors will return loan to foreigners at a higher % of interest. This will make rupee a more appealing currency to invest in, this will help its value to go up.

These measure introduced by the government will surely require time to show their effect on the rupee value. This is because higher import tax will not immediately reduce imports, or countries won't promptly buy Indian exports. Foreign investors will take time to trust that Indians return loans on time. In my opinion the government should try to make some short-term measures to help solve this situation. The short-term measure which I propose to India is; promote tourism in India. If tourism in India is promoted well across the globe, then more tourists will be willing to come to India for holidays, this will help increase cash inflow in India. Tourism doesn't need any special needs, such as factories or government initiatives, so it isn't a strenuous task to promote.

ePrabhavnomics blog 10
Originally Published on: 11 November 2018

What is the economics behind wars?

Have you ever wondered if there is any correlation between wars and economics? Do wars take place for any economics reason, such as the want for more basic necessities? If you have any questions like this then today I will be answering them in this blog, and taking about war, today (11/11/2018), 100 years have elapsed after the end of WW1. Therefore if you are able to, during the day observe a moment of silence to commemorate the soldiers that died fighting for their country. And let's hope this planet never sees such wars again. Without further ado lets starts the blog.

As I mentioned in the introduction, wars are caused for basic necessities, such as food (not just food, but any necessity). Causes of conflict for such basic necessities is; poverty, inequality, huge unemployment, economic recession (an economy is in recession if its growth rate is negative for more than 3 quarters of a year), although all these factors contribute to wars, the extent to which they contribute varies over time. These conflicts are usually between two 'less economically developed countries.'

War can be caused also due to the desire to have more valuable resources in the country, diamond and gold are examples of such resources. Countries that are willing to have such resources but unable to mine/produce them can be having such conflicts with countries that do have the resources. Greed is a factor that is causing these wars, but also some need for these resources can trigger wars. For example there have been many conflicts for oil, such as the US-Iraq war between 2003 and 2011. With Iraq being the country with the oil.

The want to gain more land can also cause disputes between countries. A good example of a territorial conflict is the Kashmir conflict, between India and Pakistan. China has occasionally been part of this conflict, and currently controls 20% of Kashmir, mostly the uninhabited areas. India has control 43% of the state and Pakistan has 37% of Kashmir. This war started in 1947, and still hasn't terminated. Another instance of a war over land is, the Palestine conflict, between the State of Palestine and the State of Israel. Since the commencement commencement of the war, Palestine has been losing power over its land and Israel has snatched away all the land from Palestine.

The current civil war in Syria, that erupted in 2011 was caused due to the civilians of the country being unhappy with the President. Before the commencing of the war, many Syrians were complaining about there being high unemployment, corruption and lack of political freedom under President Bashar al-Assad. Therefore you can see, how discontent with the countries' government can also lead to huge civil wars.

Overall, from these four paragraphs we can see that what usually triggers wars is scarcity. Wars do cause the overall GDP (gross domestic product- total goods and services produced by a country in a year) to plummet, but the greed to become more prosperous, or even the lack of basic necessities makes people want to initiate a conflict with others. As I said in the introduction let's all hope to not see wars on this planet again, and let's promote peace.

ePrabhavnomics blog 11

Originally Published on: 18 November 2018

What are the economic factors that shaped WW1?

As you may know, last Sunday was Armistice Day, 100 years passed after end of WW1. After my last blog I decided I should write a blog dedicated to WW1, and the economic factors that shaped it. Last week's blog was on the economics behind war, but every war is caused due to different economic factors, and this blog will show the ones of WW1, and I will also talk about how each of these factors could have worked as advantages for some countries.

The factor we will be looking at is size. The Allies, which include countries like; Britain, France, Russia and the United States, have a overwhelming size advantage in terms of both population and production (weaponry, tanks and planes). But sadly due to them mismanaging this advantage, they weren't able to win as swiftly as they could have, if they utilised this advantage of size properly. Although at the end of the day, quantity helped the Allies to a large extent.

Apart from quantity of the resources their quality mattered more, and the main factor affecting their quality was the amount of development made by a country when NOT in war, this is also known as peacetime development. The amount of development made can be measured using the average income per capita. Wealthier countries were able to make better use of the resources, able to get higher public taxes, and prepare soldier and weaponry more efficiently. Overall, prosperity of the country aided in accumulating more resources for war. The number of connections a country had to foreign markets, also mattered in this scenario. For example although Britain had control of most of Africa, most of Africa was barren, therefore this wasn't a colossal advantage to Britain. Instead US had access to more rich markets, giving it an upper hand in war.

Some countries like; Austria-Hungary, Turkey, Germany and Russia (Central Powers) finished their supply of food much before having terminated their quantity of guns and shells, because they were highly dependent on imports, as a war strategy the British navy stopped them from importing, so dependency on domestic farming increased. During wartime the focus on farming in these countries was plummeting, and the motivation for farmers to grow food was reduced. Due to this many farmers started producing only for their families, the economy then started to disintegrate. As war progressed the market supply of food dried up in these countries. Food prices started to soar and urban famine commenced.

On the other hand countries like Britain, that were forecasted to starve, as these countries were highly depended on food imports, managed the situation adequately, British farmers were offered higher prices, and this incentive helped them boost their production. Higher productivity of farm labour also meant that, there was a chances of expanding output of other resources as well.

To conclude in WW1, both the quantity and quality of the resources a country owned mattered. The level of economic development was crucial in organising the troops and weaponry for war. From what happened to the Central Powers we can also see that, for war the production of necessities couldn't come to a standstill. Due to the terrible economic condition of the Central Powers, the Allies had the chance to dominate over them.

ePrabhavnomics blog 12

Originally Published on: 25 November 2018

The economic impacts due to climate change

Climate change is the result of increasing levels of carbon dioxide and other greenhouse gases in the Earth's atmosphere. The greenhouse gases trap heat from the sun, this has lead to a 0.7C increase in the Earth's temperature in the last 40 years. Many scientists agree that humans are a leading factor in climate change. Income of a person and their contribution to climate change is proportional, a recent study said that the wealthiest 1 billion people contributes to 60% of greenhouse gases, while the poorest 3 billion people produced only 5%. I have spoken about the basics of climate change, so now I will move to the main topic of the blog, the economic effects of climate change, which are mostly negative but there is one positive effect of climate change. So without further ado let's start with these effects.

Firstly due to climate change there is mass forced migration around the world, this is also called 'environmental migration'. For example, due to rising sea levels, many people prefer to leave places that are vulnerable to floods. These migrants may find it difficult to witness a better quality of life in their place of destination, and may face huge poverty. If they migrate internationally, the government of the new country will be put on strain, as they will have to spend more on looking after the unexpected new arrivals, this will lead to an opportunity cost, because the government won't be able to focus on different aspects of development in the country.

The agricultural industry will be affected by two extreme weather events; droughts and floods. Both these events happen unexpectedly and will lead to decrease in agricultural production. Due to this, the quantity of food available on the planet to feed everyone will be lower and food prices will soar. If incomes don't rise at the same rate as food price do, fewer people can afford it, poverty rate will rise due to this. If lower production leads to lower revenue, firms will have to lay-off workers, so that they don't have to spend their revenue on wages of workers, unemployment will prevail.

Acid rain can also prove to be detrimental to some industries, such as fisheries. Acid rain will pollute the oceans, killing marine life. This will lead to lower production of fisheries, and will cause a dip in the incomes and revenue of the fisherman. Acid rain can also negatively affect farms, as all the soil will become infertile.

'Less economically developed countries' (LEDCs) are the most affected by disasters caused by extreme weather events. Due to poor infrastructure, these disasters easily damage it, this also increases the citizens' exposure to these calamities. The government will have to spend lots on repairing the infrastructure and on health care, as greater exposure will lead to several injuries and deaths in the country. The government may not even have enough revenue to bear these losses, therefore it may have to borrow from other countries, leading to a debt.

And now the positive effect of climate change; the melting of ice in the poles can open up a passage of water which ships can travel trough when importing/exporting goods, this passage is a shortcut for the ships. Ships weren't able to travel trough that passage previously, as it was covered in ice. An example of this happening is the opening of the North West Passage, which connects the Atlantic and Pacific oceans through the Canadian Archipelago. This shortcut has not only helped reduce travel time of ships, but has also helped save $800,000 in fuel costs annually, and increased 25% cargo.

Overall, it can be seen that climate change bring mostly negative effects on the economy. Scientists of many countries are researching on finding water on other planets, I feel that instead if we protect our glaciers from melting, or the melting glacier water to run in to the seas, we may find the solution for the depleting water resources, I believe protecting resources on our planet is easier than finding resources on other planets. Apart from that, there are abundant methods to cause the rate of climate change to dip. For example we ourselves can reduce carbon dioxide emissions by; taking public transport, riding a bike, car-sharing, using hybrid vehicle, at home we can do our bit by switching electrical instruments when not using them, instead of craving for exotic food from far way countries eating zeroKM food. Eager to know your views.

ePrabhavnomics blog 13
Originally Published on: 2 December 2018

The UN and economic development

Have any of you ever wondered if the UN influences economic development or not? If yes, then how? If you ever had such questions in mind, then this blog will answer all of them. Plus, this blog will also be talking about the history of the UN and why it was formed? So without further ado let's start this blog, and see how the UN and economic development are correlated.

The UN is the acronym for the United Nations, and it was formed on 24 October 1945, post WW2. It is an intergovernmental organisation (an organisation that is composed of mainly sovereign states), which's task is to maintain international peace and security, to help develop friendly relations among nations, to achieve internal co-operation and be the centre for co-ordinating the action of nations. It has it's headquarters in Manhattan, New York City, it also has some of its main offices in places like: Geneva, Nairobi and Vienna. The UN has 193 members. The UN is the substitute of the unsuccessful 'League of Nations', which had a similar task as the UN.

Now let's look at how it influences economic development. In the year 2000, the UN formed 8 goals called 'Millennium Development Goals' (MDGs), and world leaders had committed their countries into achieving these goals by 2015. Some of these goals included: halving extreme, to terminate the spread of HIV/AIDs and to provide primary education. And there were different initiatives launched by the Secretary General to attain these goals, such as: 'Zero Hunger' Challenge and 'Every Woman, Every Child'. And already lots of progress has been made into achieving this goals such as; the percentage of people living below $1.90 a day dropped from 31% in 2000 to 9.6% in 2015. The global maternal mortality ratio fell by 37% from 2000 to 2015, under-5 mortality rate fell by 44%. 2000 to 2015 saw a 46% reduction in HIV cases, 17% dip in tuberculosis cases and 41% decline in malaria cases. Well, we have made lots of progress but still have a colossal amount left to improve. So overall we can say that, these goals have helped the economy get better, and grow.

After the MDGs showed success, by 2015 there were more serious issue in the world, such as climate change (as it was showing its effect faster). Therefore the UN's Secretary-General devised 17 'Sustainable Development Goals' (SDGs), these 17 gaols were made to complete the work which the MDGs had commenced, and these goals were expected to be achieved by 2030.

The SDGs include to many aspects of development to make the world a better place. One example is climate change, and it aims to limit the temperature rise to below 1.5C. It also aims to create quality city infrastructure, such as resilient buildings, so that natural disasters cause less damage to communities, and will cause lower number of deaths/injuries. To ensure gender equality and empower women and girls, albeit the fact that MDGs have helped gender equality to improve, huge number of women and girls still suffer from violence worldwide. UN women are working to eradicate this violence, and to empower women and girls.

Overall, it can be concluded that the UN has aided the world in becoming a better place to live. In my personal opinion, without these goals being imposed, the today the world would have been worse than what it is in the present situation. The world is making progress to reach the goals, but I think more is needed in order to fulfil them. I personally feel it could take beyond 2030 to realise them, for example because of speedy population growth (note; percentage wise growth rate may be low, but actual figure wise it is high, as the world have humongous number of people). But let's all be bit optimistic and hope for the best, and that the goals will be realised at the earliest.

Eager to know your opinions, when will these goals be fulfilled according to you?

ePrabhavnomics blog 14
Originally Published on: 9 December 2018

Possible solutions to solve income inequality

Income inequality is a major issue the world is currently facing. Currently the richest 1% (those with more than $1 million) of the world's population owns 45% of the world's total wealth, meanwhile the poorest 64% (those with less than $10 thousand) own only 2% of the world's total wealth. As I mentioned in my last blog, the 'Sustainable Development Goals' are made to make the world a better place, and one of the goals is 'Reduced Inequality'. So, in this blog I will be suggesting some ways in which we can reduce/end income inequality. Without much further ado, let's start the blog.

Firstly the government should increase the minimum wage in the country. A minimum wage is a wage which workers cannot be payed below. For example in the US the minimum wage is $7.25 per hour, this means that it is illegal to pay a worker in the US an amount below $7.25 per hour. Developing countries in the world do have a minimum wage, although it is minuscule, therefore it's effect isn't felt in the country. If it is set at a reasonable rate, at which every worker is able to afford basic necessities, in the long-run it can help to alleviate poverty in the country. Setting a minimum wage won't affect economic growth.

Raise the taxes on high income workers, and lower them for low income workers. The government by doing this, can reduce the spending power of the wealthy, and they can invest this extra tax revenue in helping the poor, in areas such as education. As mentioned in the last paragraph if the government is able to get the underprivileged a proper education, they will get higher pay. What the government can do to help improve education percentage between these people, is build more schools, purchase extra school supply, like books.

Invest in education. The government can increase investment in education, especially in developing areas of the country. One of the main reasons for income inequality is due to the differences in education levels, and education quality. In many developing countries a tiny percentage of the population is able to go to school and get an education, and even if they do get an education, a small amount of it is quality education. This leads to the population have limited skills, thus they become part of the unskilled labour (jobs examples; cleaners, hotel maids). As barely any skills and qualifications are required to do jobs, an enormous percentage of the population can do those jobs, supply is greater than demand, so price (wages) is lower. In conclusion, if quality and quantity of education is high in the country, a greater portion of the population will get the chance to do high-skilled jobs and therefore will receive an additional pay.

Apart from just investing in education and giving the workers more skills, the government has to look at which sectors of the economy need more attention. For example most African and developing countries have a colossal amount of their GDP in agriculture, therefore they need more workers there. The government therefore needs to make sure greater number of workers get education about agriculture.

Men are paid 30% more than women who do the same job, this is prevalent in every place around the world. This is mainly due to the lots of gender stereotypes, that women shouldn't go to work and look after the house. Women have decided to start to work, but usually take long breaks when on maternity, so if the government decides to invest more in nurseries, children will be taken care of there, and so women can stay in work.

Overall, these are my possible solutions to solve income inequality around the globe, if any of you have any suggestion then definitely let me know. I hope that the governments understands this issue and takes measures drastically, because unfortunately at the current scenario the richer are getting richer and poorer getting poorer.

ePrabhavnomics blog 15
Originally Published on: 16 December 2018

Possible ways to increase literacy rate for sustainable economic development

Illiteracy is a huge problem around the world, especially in developing countries. Even today globally approximately 750 million people aged above 15 are still unable to read and write, with 2/3 of this population being women. As mentioned in my previous blog, an improved literacy rate will enable workers to get high skilled jobs, and thus they get better pay. Also more workers being part of skilled labour, will increase the country's productivity. In this blog I will be giving some possible solutions to help improve the global literacy rate.

So firstly, the wealthy population should support and fund literacy programs. Literacy programs are initiatives to help the least literate to improve their reading and writing skills, and to achieve this goal they do the following; provide educational resources to students and teachers, give extra training to teachers and build basic infrastructure for education. If the rest of the population helps by funding and supporting these schemes, the organisers will be more incentivised to work on them and carry them forward. If the progress made by them is constant, they will definitely help to reduce illiteracy around the globe, but it will take a long period of time and tonnes of effort.

Encourage adult literacy programs, note that in the previous paragraph I was talking about programs to aid children. As stated in the introduction around 750 million people over 15 years old are illiterate, while only 126 million people under 15 are illiterate. If parents don't have basic education and knowledge their children won't be much incentivised to go to school and get education. And if elders have greater insight, their quality of life will rise, because if they are still working they can shift to a more skilled job and earn more. With more of the working population doing skilled labour it will also increase the economy's productivity and creativity.

Focus mostly on subsiding female aiding programs. Global female literacy is 82.7%, while male literacy is 90%, and in MOST countries male literacy is higher than female literacy. If income inequality between genders is to be reduced, additional females should join the labour force. Literacy is the key to getting a better job and pay, as greater knowledge will lead to more skills and higher salary. Incentivising female literacy programs will cause the inequality to plummet rapidly, and help women empowerment. Also women will have more knowledge about basic hygiene and health about children and childbirth. Raised literacy will also cause childbirth to reduce, as women will be more aware of contraception, and overall world population will be in control.

Donate books and other material to charities. Although as stated in the second paragraph, the literacy programs provide educational resources to students and teachers, the society can help by donating their own material, which they don't utilise anymore. This will aid the programs to advance, and the underprivileged will receive more educational material for themselves, so their betterment in learning to read and write will be swifter.

Overall, from this blog it can be understood that we should aid this change, there are abundant number of organisations trying to address this issue, but we should also be part of bringing this transformation. And if the organisations get larger incentive, they will be encouraged to improve. The good news is that the global literacy rate is continuously rising, in 2000 it was 81.5% and in 2016 it was 86.25%. The percentage increase may seem little, but taking into account the world population, the actual number of people that become literate in this period is colossal. Let's hope this upward trend continues and the world is able to achieve 100% literacy, and remember to do give your share in this, even if it is the smallest.

ePrabhavnomics blog 16
Originally Published on: 23 December 2018

Does the geographical location of a country influence its economic development?

There are many components that decide how economically developed a country is. One of them is the geographical location of the country, yes, some countries are richer than others due to differences in location. In this blog I will be explaining which location variations have influenced development and will then give some examples of countries affected. Before starting I would like to state that, if you are currently thinking of something like this right now, 'a country's geographic location will always remain the same, so will the country always remain impoverished', then I will say that, there could be possible solutions to overcome this problem, which I will mention in this blog.

Firstly, a country's access to foreign markets is important in deciding how developed it is. The greater number of connections a country has, the easier it is for that country to trade. Trade is important because, every country cannot produce all the goods required by the population, so trade can help to reduce scarcity of goods to some extent. Countries with poor access to foreign markets are the least developed ones, for example South America has two landlocked countries, Bolivia and Paraguay, and they are poorest countries in the continent. Coming to Africa, it has 15 landlocked countries, out of which 11 have a per capita income of $600 or less. Afghanistan is the poorest country in Asia, and is also landlocked. A solution for underprivileged landlocked countries to develop is that; they can study the needs and wants of their citizens, and work on producing greater amount of those goods. This way these countries will reduce dependency on imports.

There are some exceptions to this, for example Switzerland is landlocked, but is still the 2nd wealthiest country, according to the 'Human Development Index' (HDI). This could be because of Switzerland having prosperous neighbouring countries, and its relatively small population.

Secondly, latitude of the country determines its prosperity. Latitude tells how north/south a country is from the equator. Latitude is measured in degrees, with 0° being the equator and 90° being the north/south poles. The underdeveloped countries have a latitude between 15°N and 15°S. This is because countries located here have very hot and humid climates. This leads to land being infertile and a very limited water resource, making agricultural production dip. Due to hot and humid climate, nations near the equator are also exposed to many tropical diseases such as; dengue, yellow fever, ebola, TB to name a few. All 'less economically developed countries' simultaneously face 5 tropical diseases. The countries facing such problems can look at how they can improve their health care system, this way even if the population gets a disease, it can be easily treated.

A country's risk to natural disasters, such as floods, earthquakes, tsunamis. Although the correlation between amount of risk to natural disasters and development of the country is not direct, but the amount of destruction made by the disaster is inversely proportional to the development of the nation. Wealthier nations are able to react swifter when compared to underprivileged ones. For example if we compare the earthquake in Kobe, Japan (1995) and that in Haiti (2010), then we can see that although Kobe has a slightly stronger earthquake, its effects were lower than that in Haiti, and it took less amount of time to recover from the earthquake in Kobe. Bangladesh which is also a 'less economically developed country' faces huge flooding, a stronger infrastructure (for example: stronger houses) would help minimise the floods' effects.

The availability of natural resources and how efficiently they are utilised by the country. For example, Saudi Arabia and UAE are the most oil rich countries, and exporting the oil allows them to make colossal amount of money. South Africa, one of the richest countries in Africa has a humungous quantity of gold and diamonds. The Democratic Republic of Congo is rich in coltan, but due to the nation having weak institutions, it is unable to take advantage of this upper-hand.

Overall, geography hugely establishes how developed a country is to a huge extent. As said in the introduction, although countries have their location as their disadvantage, they can still overcome this drawback. In this blog the solutions I proposed were, that the countries develop their infrastructure, this will help them become a prosperous country albeit their geographical disadvantage.

ePrabhavnomics blog 17
Originally Published on: 30 December 2018

Major economic events that took place in 2018

2018 is about to end, and as we enter in the New Year, let us look back at how the year about to close has passed. So today, being my last blog of 2018, I will be writing about few major economic events that took place this year. These events aren't in any particular order, they are just the ones which I believe shaped the world in the year. Before starting I would just like to mention that 2018 marked the 100th anniversary of the end of World War 1, on November 11. The reason why I stated this anniversary was because WW1 impacted the global economy in a negative way, leaving many countries in debt and hyperinflation.

In March this year, Italy elected it's new Prime Minister. The new government wants to increase their public spending to 2.4% of their GDP (0.8% last government's spending), because they would like to increase unemployment benefits and improve pensions. This was beyond the EU's permissible levels of 2%, therefore Italy is in risk of getting sanctions from the EU. The government is unwilling to reduce the spending levels, therefore this will lead to Italy's economy to decline. Italy already has an alarming rate of EU debts (131% of the GDP).

In July, India became the 6th largest economy in the world, after overtaking France. At the time of overtaking India's Gross Domestic Product was US$2.59 trillion, and France's was US$2.58 trillion. India is also expected to surpass the 5th largest economy, which is the UK (US$2.62 trillion), very soon. This is a major achievement as it shows India's rapid economic growth, and India as a possible economic giant in the future.

Also in July, the trade war between US and China commenced. The US imposed taxes on exports to China, due to this China was affected, as most of its imports were from US. China reacted by doing the same to US (placing tariffs on exports to the US). These two countries were major trading partners, thus a sudden decline in trade between the two hit both economies badly. On the good side countries like India, which have to increase their exports, can take advantage of this situation and start to produce more goods required by these two countries, and thus that country will be able to increase their exports.

In October around 700,000 people in London protested to have a second vote on Brexit. Brexit will mean that Britain no longer has the same rights as the other European Union countries. For example the UK wouldn't be able to trade it's good to other EU members without having to pay a tariff. This will make British goods dearer and less competitive, when compared to the exports of other EU countries. Brexit will be pessimistic for the UK, therefore this protest was to re-vote on whether to leave or stay.

This incident took place for several weekends in November and December, and on a side note I witnessed it; it was the Paris 'yellow vests' Riots. These riots took place in the centre of Paris, where people were wearing 'yellow vests' and protesting the rise in gas and diesel prices. The city was in chaos, with cars being burnt, many important ruins being destroyed, and hundreds of injuries taking place. The reason why this event was significant was because, petrol is a necessity for the citizens, and an increase in its price, causes its affordability to dip.

In Venezuela there has been a huge humanitarian crisis, going on for several years, 2018 being one of the years when this crisis was worst. After Venezuela went in recession (a period when economic growth is negative), the government was unable to revive the economy. Many industries are failing during this period, for example the health care industry lacks many resources, thus causing infant mortality and maternal mortality to significantly rise. Disease burden and poverty in the country has also spiked. Venezuela is an oil rich country, with 90% of its export earnings being oil. The country however is unable to take full advantage of this, and this is why it is facing a downfall.

So in conclusion, these are the few economic incidents that I believe were significant in 2018. If you think I have missed out some, then definitely let me know. Hope you all had a wonderful 2018, and wishing you a happy and prosperous 2019. There are many crucial economic events that are expected to take place in the coming year, which I will be talking about in my next blog.

ePrabhavnomics blog 18
Originally Published on: 6 January 2019

Major economic events expected to take place in 2019

2019 has begun, and just like every year, this year is also expected to have many significant events taking place. So in this blog, I will be writing about the major economic events one can expect in this new year. There will obviously many more events taking place than listed in the blog, these are just the major ones. Before starting I would like to wish everyone a Happy New Year!

On 29 March the UK will be leaving the EU. As you may know on 23 June 2016, there was a referendum in which people voted on whether the UK should remain in the EU or leave it. The 'leave' outnumbered the 'remain', with 51.9% to 48.1%. As mentioned in my previous blog, the UK might suffer from Brexit, as it doesn't have the same rights as the other EU members. The UK will leave the EU using the 'Article 50', a law which allows an EU member to withdraw, in accordance with its constitutional (the way the government works) requirements. The UK cannot avoid Brexit, although it can be delayed with the UK extending 'Article 50', if the UK leaders are confident that the UK can end up remaining a member of the EU. The UK might have to go through another referendum. Overall this is a complicated process, that will definitely take several months, and looks unlikely.

From 26 March to 7 April India will have a prime minister election, the current prime minster of India (note: I don't want to write people's names in my blog) who started his term in 2014, has helped India develop. He has tackled many issues in the country such as; inflation, corruption, poverty, and unemployment to name a few. One of his biggest schemes took place on 8 November 2016, and it was the banning of notes, to eradicate black money in the country. So overall, he has aided the country's growth, and there are high hopes by the population that he will be re-elected. I too hope for him being re-elected, because he has done his job with complete perfection in his first-term, and I am confident he will do so even in his second-term. On 25 May the term will commence for the prime minister, and the next elections will be in 2024.

Apart from India, there are many other countries that will hold elections in 2019. They are as follows; Nigeria- Parliament members and president (16 February). Israel- Parliament (9 April). Indonesia- All levels of the government (17 April). Afghanistan- President (20 April). EU- Parliament (23-26 May). Also there has already been a presidential election in Brazil on 1 January. The results of the elections will massively influence the economies of the country and overall of the globe. The EU Parliament election will be the most important one, since it is the first one to take place after UK's exit from the EU.

About 3/4 of the top economies will experience a slowdown in growth. Already last year there were many economies that started experiencing a drop in growth. For example Japan and Germany's economies shrank in the last quarter. Although every country's cause for going into recession is different, trade wars is a common factor in causing recession in these economies. Trade wars decrease exports and imports in countries, so the country has fewer goods and services in the market. If many major countries face slowdowns, the US will suffer as well, because the US relies on goods from foreign countries and doing business with them will become more difficult.

Apart from this 2019 has many events both economic ones and non-economic ones as well. The dates of these events may change due to some reasons, currently unknown or many unexpected events could occur over the course of the year. These are just some which I believe are important and could change the world positively or negatively. If there are any events which you think I missed out, then feel free to let me know.

ePrabhavnomics blog 19
Originally Published on: 13 January 2019

Influence of taxes on the economy

The government levies taxes for several reasons, mainly so that the government gets greater revenue and utilising this revenue can invest in the country's development. Taxes therefore is vital in the economy, and also affects the economy, the government can impose two different types of taxes; direct and indirect taxes. Directs taxes is when the government directly places taxes on your incomes, meanwhile indirect taxes is when the government raises the price of a good or service to discourage its excess use, for example cigarettes. Direct taxes have both short and long term effects on the economy.

Starting with the short run effects, a reduction in tax will cause aggregate demand (total demand for good and services in the economy) to increase, this is due to consumers having greater disposable income (income left after subtracting taxes and social security charges). Tax reduction will also increase business investment, like they can buy new machinery/technology, thus possibly allowing them to become more efficient, and so increase production in the economy. Meanwhile if taxes are raised, the opposite effect will be faced. So, if at time of tax increase the economy is performing poorly the impact will be huge, this is because when the economy is in recession the total 'gross domestic product'. (GDP- total goods/services produced) tend to plummet, and therefore income falls too, so higher taxes will be unfavourable to the mass. Meanwhile, if the economy is running at full capacity (making use of its available resources to produce its maximum, in a specific period of time), the increase will impact the economy minimally. And obviously the opposite if tax is reduced.

Coming to the long run effects, if taxes are low, the government may face a budget deficit (govt spending higher than govt revenue) in the long run, this is because they wouldn't have collected enough from the population, and this may hinder the development of the economy as the government has little amount of budget from which they can invest in the country's infrastructure development. While with high taxes, the workers can be affected negatively if income levels aren't as high as taxes. If income levels remain lower than tax rates during a period of time, the affordability levels of the population will shrink. Therefore overall, we can conclude that in the long run, both very high taxes and also very low taxes will influence the economy's progress.

As said in the introduction indirect taxes are placed to reduce demand for particular goods and services, and is an increase in that good/service's price. With these types of taxes, the government tax revenue raises. If the government places taxes also on the material required to produce those goods, the producers of those goods produce less of them, since the production cost has increased due to the indirect tax. The producers in order to not lose any revenue will raise the price of that good, a higher price will deter consumers from buying that product. Overall this will help reduce social costs (costs to the society due to a transaction), like for example if there are less smokers, the costs faced by passive smoking will be reduce. Fewer social costs will mean less market failure (when the price mechanism leads to inefficient resource allocation), thus more economic efficiency. Although, all this will depend on price elasticity of demand for the good, which means 'the responsiveness of quantity demanded to a change in price', so there might be some goods which despite price rise might not see a huge decrease in demand (low price elasticity of demand- price inelastic), while some goods even a negligible price rise could cause its demand to drastically fall (high price elasticity of demand- price elastic). So if the good with the indirect tax has a low price elasticity of demand, the consumption of that good will only vaguely fall, thus making the tax seem useless.

Overall, the short run effects of the taxes is dependent on; size of tax, economic performance at time of tax change and whether tax was raised or reduced. Meanwhile in the longer run the taxes shouldn't be nor too high nor too low, cause this can affect either the government or the common population. An indirect taxes will help reduce market failure, but only if the demand for the good is price elastic, and consumers stop consuming the good after the price increment. In conclusion from all this it can be seen that there are many conditions that need to be determined to know how exactly a tax will influence the economy.

ePrabhavnomics blog 20
Originally Published on: 20 January 2019

The economic impacts of migration

Migration is very common, every second a person leaves a country and enters another one. Migration can be permanent or temporary and it can also be forced (refugees) or voluntary. The main purpose of voluntary migration is to find a better lifestyle (better health, pay and education), therefore migration usually takes place with someone leaving a 'less economically developed country' (LEDC) and entering a 'more economically developed country' (MEDC). Migration hugely influences the economy either positively or negatively. So in this blog I will be explaining how immigration (a person entering a country) and emigration (a person leaving a country), and how both of them have positive and negative effects on the country of origin/destination's economy.

Before beginning the blog I would like to give the definition of 4 words which I will use quite commonly in the blog: immigration, emigration, migration and migrants.

Immigration is the act of a person entering a country. Emigration is the act of a person exiting a country. Migration is the general term used for the act of people moving from one place to another. Migrants are those people who have moved to another country, and are not residing in their local country.

So let's start with positive effects of immigration on the economy. If a country is facing a labour shortage, an immigration of skilled labour can hugely help the country in solving the labour shortage, thus the total production of the country will increase and thus also the 'Gross Domestic Product' (GDP), a higher GDP means that the per capita income of the country will also see a rise. The government will be able to collect a greater tax revenue from incomes, they can then spend this extra revenue in helping the country's development. The increase in workforce will mean the country's dependency ratio (how many workers have to look after the non-working population, which is both young people and old ones) will decrease, meaning less pressure on the working population.

Immigration can also make the economy face some negative effects. For example, if there are very few job vacancies, migrants won't help contribute to the labour force, instead unemployment will rise, or if the migrants don't have those skills/qualifications which the country of destination needs, then their use will be minimal. Immigration causes an increase in the country's population, therefore a huge amount of immigration could lead to the country facing overpopulation, which means there are too many people for the amount of food and other basic necessities available, this will cause poverty levels to spike. The migrants themselves may also face negative consequences, as they may be exploited by locals and become part of the cheap labour, this is a disadvantage for the migrants because they aren't unable to make full use of their qualifications. If the migrants aren't given the opportunity to utilise their skills to the fullest, then the economy's production many not increase, and if the country is facing a labour shortage, then production might also decline, and the economy may go in recession.

Moving on to emigration, the positive effects are; if the country is facing overpopulation then huge emigration could reduce pressure on basic necessities. Unemployment will also see a dip, if the migrants are workers. Remittances can help the country of origin, a remittance is 'money sent by migrants to the country of origin'. If the country of origin is a LEDC then remittances can aid the country to develop rapidly, this is because the money acts as a fund for the country of origin, and this 'fund' can be utilised for helping the country's development. It is possible that the migrants which are part of the working force may return to the country of origin with more skills, this will therefore be an advantage to the that country.

Emigration also causes an economy to face negative effects, if majority of the emigrants are part of the working population then the economy may face a labour shortage in the longer run, if immigration of workers is lower than emigration. The country will lose its talented workers, and another country will benefit from those workers' talent (called brain-drain).

Overall, migration causes both benefits and drawbacks to the country of origin/destination. These downsides can be overcome if migrants aren't exploited by the local population, but instead are given their due in foreign countries, and if the governments of LEDCs manages to give their citizens a great quality of life then fewer locals will feel like emigrating.

ePrabhavnomics blog 21
Originally Published on: 27 January 2019

Economic impacts of urbanisation

Last week's blog was on 'International Migration', meaning migration from one country to another, this week I will be looking at 'National Migration', which is migration within a country, and the most common type of national migration is 'Urbanisation'. Urbanisation is the process of people migrating from rural areas (the countryside) to urban areas (cities), when people living in rural areas reach middle class status and are searching for a better lifestyle (better paid jobs, better education for children and better health care facilities), they shift to urban areas. Every year 77 million people move from rural to urban areas, and urbanisation is taking place in every country. Due to urbanisation number of megacities in the world has increased drastically, a megacity is a city with more than 10 million people.

Back in 1950 the world hosted only 2 megacities; Tokyo and New York, but with rapid urbanisation this number has risen to 33 today, with China being home to 6 and India having 4. In this blog I will be focusing on the economic impacts faced due to urbanisation and will be focusing mainly on megacities, and its positive and negative economic impacts.

Urbanisation mainly helps the people who have migrated, although it does help the economy of the country as well. As mentioned in the introduction in urban areas citizens have more access to education, basic necessities like food, water, health care and sanitation. Better access to education will help youth literacy to increase, so a highly skilled workforce in the future. It will also help the current workforce coming from rural areas to improve their skills, helping the current labour force of the country to be more efficient, as a result higher national output, leading to higher income for workers. Higher income for all workers will reduce the country's income inequality. Transport and communication is also better in urban areas, which makes commuting easy, workers can work even longer, and thus produce more output.

Although urbanisation does help improve quality of life of middle-income people, it also has many negative effects, both on the economy and the individuals. This negative effects faced by urbanisation are mostly prevalent in 'less economically developed countries' (LEDCs). About 1/3 of the urban population LEDCs lives in slums, and as many people know, residents of slums have to face poor living conditions, like overcrowding, poor access to services (health care and education). Rapid urbanisation leads to vehicles on the streets, causing an increase in both air pollution and traffic congestion in the city. This will affect the health of the residents in the city, this means that the economy's efficiency has declined, and will strain the government into finding a solution to avoid this problem in the future.

Most of the output produced by LEDCs comes from agriculture and farming, therefore with rapid urbanisation in LEDCs most of the agricultural workers are lost, thus agriculture production dips.

Apart from this, agricultural land could be cut off to make way for; new houses, factories or any other important building, this also causes food production to plummet, possibly causing poverty rates in the country to spike.

On the whole, urbanisation does both have benefits and costs to the economy. Urbanisation is inevitable, because those living in rural areas wants to find a better lifestyle by moving to urban areas. Costs of urbanisation can be managed if; the government is able to build adequate infrastructure in urban areas to support the growing population and if there are subsidies to products produced in rural areas, this way there is less chance of those products facing shortages in the future.

ePrabhavnomics blog 22

Originally Published on: 3 February 2019

Economic impacts of tourism

In the last two blogs I have been exploring the economic impacts of migration (international and national- urbanisation), both these migrations were long-term. In this blog I will be looking again at international migration, but this time short-term, which is tourism. I will be looking at what are the economic impacts of tourism, in the country of destination. There are both positive and negative impacts of tourism on the country of destination.

Beginning with the positive impacts, higher number of tourists arriving in the country, will help generate jobs for locals. This is because more tourists entering the country means, more employees will be needed to manage the tourist services, like hotels or popular sights. The money which tourists use to pay for services, for example hotels, get added to the country's economy. This extra money will lead to the country's economic growth. Many countries' gross domestic product (GDP- total amount of goods + services produced by a country annually) consists of tourism, for example 76.6% of Maldives' economy consists of tourism, which is the highest for any country. Seychelles is in 2nd place with 65.3% of its GDP consisting of tourism. When firms which manage tourists receive pay from tourists, the revenue can be used as income for the employees in that firm, therefore higher number of tourists will mean greater income for the employees. Many small business can grow due to mass tourism, small businesses include: taxi services, souvenir shops and small restaurants. Tourist will use these services more than local people do, therefore even here greater number of tourists increases the amount of cash received by these small businesses. Overall greater tourism in a country helps the country to generate more revenue, the extra revenue leads to economic growth and greater income.

Coming to the negative impacts, if number of tourist arriving is greater than the infrastructure can sustain, the tourism industry will need to raise the price of its services to dis-incentivise many tourists from arriving in the country. Apart from just dis-incentivising tourists from arriving in the country, a price increase also causes the affordability of these services among locals to decrease, in short the country faces inflation. An example of dis-incentivising tourists is a car free zone in Zermatt, Switzerland, which makes reaching to the destination difficult especially with toddlers or elderly. Another negative impacts could be, tourists might be unaware of the importance of many heritage sights in the country, they might mistreat these sights, putting the burden on the locals and the govt. on the restoration of damages caused by tourists. The government will have to invest most of its resources in touristic activities, therefore will forgo investment in other areas of the country that really need investment. Over-depending on tourism could be imprudent for the economy, since tourism could also fall over the years, this will then cause the economy to face hurdles. A country therefore has to balance between goods/services production and tourism. Here we can conclude that tourism affects the locals as well as the economy.

There are some touristic activities that are seasonal, such as skiing in winter or going to the beach in summer. This is a disadvantage for those employed in these type of locations, because they remain unemployed during the off season, and are unable to grab the amount of yearly income that others do.

In conclusion tourism does both benefit and detriment the economy and the local people, however I believe that the costs of tourism can be averted. Ways of preventing the costs include; placing a tax on entry in the city, an example is Venice, which sees 24 million tourists every year, the Italian government has approved levying a tourist tax ranging from €2.50 to €10 per person depending on the season, this will hugely boost the country's revenue. Locals can place information boards in front of important sights that illustrate why these sights are significant to the country, along with the code of conduct inside the sights. The tourist industry can look at increasing infrastructure for the extra tourists in the country, which is very difficult, although could be done by improving national connectivity and facilitating higher quality services. The government will have to manage its budget between tourism and other areas in the economy.

ePrabhavnomics blog 23
Originally Published on: 10 February 2019

How is the total expenditure/aggregate demand in an economy calculated?

There are many activities taking place in an economy, an important one of them is expenditure. Expenditure is important for the economy since it can help the economy's GDP to rise (how will be told in the blog). Another way of saying expenditure is aggregate demand (AD), which is a sum of all expenditures within an economy, over a period of one year. There are many factors which need to be taken into account to get to the final value of AD in an economy. In this blog I will be explaining them all.

The first factor that we need to look at is 'consumption by households'. Consumption is all of the purchases which households make on final goods and services, (final refers to goods/services (GS) ready for consumption, GS can also be labelled as 'intermediate goods/services, which are GS used during the production process of final GS). I would also like to clarify a common misconception, housing (act of buying houses) is NOT consumption, it is investment. This is because consumption usually involves spending on; non-durable goods, like food, clothing and medicines. Durable goods; TVs, fridges, cars and washings machines. Also on services; education, health care and entertainment. Investment is spending on capital goods, and houses are capital goods. Levels of consumption also indicated the level of income in the economy, since higher income leads to higher consumption.

'Investment by firms' is the next factor we will be focusing on. As stated at the end of the previous paragraph, investment is the spending on capital goods and is carried out mainly by firms, capital goods are goods which are used to produce other goods. Investment can also refer to the spending done for construction of houses, buildings, or other infrastructural projects.

'Government spending' is next. This refers to spending by government within the country, at any level (local, regional, national). It also includes purchases which the government makes, and investment made by the government. Investment made by the government is named 'public investment', which is usually done on capital goods, like roads, airports, power generators, schools and hospitals.

Last factor is 'Net Trade'. This refers to the total value of all exports minus the total value of all imports. Exports are an addition to the country's total GDP (gross domestic product- total GS produced in an year), and are a source of 'earning' for firms, when other nations consume the exports. Imports are subtracted since they aren't domestic purchases, and leads to the economy giving its money to foreign firms.

So overall, total expenditure/AD of an economy is calculated with the following formula: Consumption + Investment + Govt Spending + (Exports − Imports). How will this influence the GDP? So when consumer spending rises, the firms receive extra revenue, therefore are incentivised to produce more of that GS. Meanwhile investment and government spending will help the economy develop, since firms/the government will invest in areas of the economy that needs attention. Meanwhile if exports are greater than imports, the balance of payments (BoP- money received from exports − money spend on imports) is in surplus, and when BoP is in surplus the output of exports rises, and therefore also GDP rises. The only negative point of a BoP in surplus is that, the value of the currency must be low.

ePrabhavnomics blog 24
Originally Published on: 17 February 2019

What are the government's main objectives?

The government is important for every country, since they are the ones which decide the country's laws. The government usually has targets in mind which they have an ambition to achieve as quickly as possible. Although every government's objectives are different, depending on the country's situation, every government has some common objectives. In this blog I will be explaining these similar goals. After explaining the aims I will also mention a country whose government needs to hugely prioritise this goal, and one country which doesn't need to worry too much about it.

The first goal is economic growth. Economic growth is the increase in production of goods and services in a economy over a period of time, usually one year. It is calculated using the growth in GDP (gross domestic product- which shows the total number of goods and services produced in a economy in a year). The government can judge how fast the economy is growing by looking at the percentage growth in GDP. The ideal growth rate for an economy is 3% for MEDCs (more economically developed countries) and 5% for LEDCs (less economically developed countries), any lower than that could be substandard for the economy, since the economy is not progressing quick enough to raise its citizen's living standards. Economic growth has several benefits such as; higher incomes, lower unemployment and greater investment. Higher incomes are generated since greater production means greater revenue earned by the country, therefore higher income per person. Lower unemployment and greater investment are both a result of firms being incentivised by the economic growth, this means that when the economy grows, firms will employ more workers and invest more in order for them to increase production again and cause the economy to grow even further. A country which need to focus very much on economic growth is; Venezuela which is facing an economic growth of -14%, and a country which doesn't need to worry much about economic growth is India which has an economic growth of 7.4%.

The second factor is low inflation. Inflation is a general increase in the price levels of a country, over time. Inflation reduces the purchasing power of citizens, if incomes don't rise at the same rate, since the goods/services become very expensive. A government targets to keep inflation rate at 2%. An inflation rate lower than 2% could also damage the economy, since the government/firms aren't able to earn much revenue for goods/services. A country where inflation is a huge concern is Venezuela, facing a whopping inflation rate of 2.68 million percent. Meanwhile Spain has the ideal inflation rate of 2%.

Next is full employment. Full employment is when all those in working age group are able to work. Full employment benefits the economy since; the economy can see a boost in its output, and the government doesn't have to worry about 'unemployment benefits', which is 'a sum of money which the government pays to unemployed people'. If the government doesn't need to spend money on unemployment benefits, they can invest in other parts of the economy which might need support. Full employment is unfortunately very difficult to achieve, since the number of jobs available in the country may be lower compared to the working population, therefore an employment rate of 3% is acceptable. A country facing huge unemployment is; South Africa with 27.5% of the working people out of work, and on the other end of the spectrum we have Qatar with 0.6% unemployed.

Next is stable balance of payments. Balance of payments or trade balance is the difference between the number of exports and imports in the country (exports minus imports), if a country exports more than it imports, its balance of payments is in surplus (excess). This is because when goods are exports the firms receive money from foreign, but when buying imports they have to spend money. When the economy has a balance of payments deficit (opposite of surplus), it will need to borrow money from foreign country in order to buy the imports. The country will have to repay the debt and the economic growth of the country will be hindered, since their goods aren't receiving many foreign consumers. There is no official 'ideal' number for the balance of payments to be at, but it is always better for it to be in surplus. Japan has the highest surplus with $165.78 billion. USA is facing the highest deficit with -$791,508.8 million.

Reaching income equality. This refers to how equally the income of the country is distributed amongst its citizens. This is very important for any country, since achieving income equality can help the country come out of poverty, and the citizens can enjoy better living standards. This is an issue faced in many countries, since the richest 10% earn much more than the poorest 10%. Most African countries and LEDCs should prioritise income equality, and MEDCs see a respite from huge pay gaps.

Lastly we have, protecting the environment. This includes; protecting greenery, reducing carbon emissions, saving water. Protecting the environment helps protect the planet from global warming, and helps protect the planet for the future generation. Lower pollution levels in a country can also help reduce the costs faced by the citizens like; illness, deaths. Thus leading to a healthier society, and therefore increasing chances of increased production within the economy. MEDCs usually perform well on this indicator and LEDCs mainly stagnate here.

Overall, these are the 6 government objectives which I believe are important for the government to achieve.

ePrabhavnomics blog 25

Originally Published on: 24 February 2019

History of my blogs

Hello everybody, today is my 25th consecutive blog, therefore rather than writing on a new topic, I will be summarising what I wrote in few of my previous blogs. Hope you enjoy!

I started with explaining impact of '$1= Indian rupees 1'. We saw that, although India will have some benefits of having a stronger currency such as; cheaper imports, therefore more ease in buying goods, there were also some negative effects a stronger currency had. These negative effects were dearer exports, higher labour costs and more expensive to invest in the country. Therefore overall it wasn't an ideal situation for developing country like India.

Later I wrote about different indicators to measure 'economic development' of a country, and gave examples of countries which were at the top of an indicator, and also those at the bottom of the indicators, this was blog 5. The indicators mentioned were; Life Expectancy, Infant Mortality Rate (IMR), GDP per capita, Literacy Rate, Education Index and Human Development Index (HDI). All these factors must be taken into account while measuring economic development of a country.

I touched an issue which concerns many Indians is 'why is the Indian rupee falling?' In blog 8. And explained what Indian government is doing to solve this issue, in blog 9. The main reasons for the weakening rupee is, less demand for it, this means that there are very few foreign countries buying Indian exports, and there are very little number of tourists and students going to India. Indian government is taking initiatives to help strengthen the rupee, and they are; boost exports, increase tourism and increase interest rates in India.

In blog 13 I looked at how the United Nations (UN) was important in influencing economic development. Here we saw that the UN has set 17 'Sustainable Development Goals' (SDGs) which it is aiming to achieve by 2030, and are targeted to help; improve health care, reduce inequality, end poverty, and many more. These goals have led to many different initiatives being launched by the UN to aid countries to develop. The world overall has become a better place since 2000 (when goals started), and can be said due to the UN's targets.

Migration is a major activity taking place every second, and it has many benefits and costs, they were explained in blog 20. When people migrate to a country, they give their talent to the destination country, but the country of origin loses those skills (brain-drain). The government of the country of destination will be put under pressure to provide extra basic services (food, water, housing) for the increased population, and the origin country will have less pressure for these basic services. So migration positively and negatively affects both the origin country and the destination country.

And in my previous blog (24), I explained what the government's objectives were. The government's main objectives, which I listed were; economic growth, low inflation, full employment, stable balance of payments, income equality and protecting the environment. Every government focuses on these 6 objectives, with each of them prioritising different ones, depending on the economic situation in the country at that moment.

Overall, these were some of the blogs and topics I wrote. You will be able to read the entire blogs on my profile, incase you are interested! Thanks for those who supported me during my blogs so far.

ePrabhavnomics blog 26
Originally Published on: 3 March 2019

Causes of inflation and ways to control inflation

Inflation is a general rise in price levels in a country, it is a serious issue since it causes the affordability levels in a country to fall. As mentioned in one of my previous blogs (blog 24) that one of the government's main aims is to keep the inflation rate at 2%. An inflation rate lower than 2% is also negative for the economy, since the firms earn less revenue from the goods/services sold. But what causes it in the first place? And how can it be solved? This blog will be answering both of these questions. Hope you enjoy!

One of the main causes of inflation is; higher aggregate demand (AD) (see blog 23 to know more about this), which is the sum of demand for ALL goods and services in an economy during a period of time, mainly caused due to; rise in income or decrease in government taxation. The aggregate supply (AS- the total supply of goods and services in the economy during a period of time) may not increase as fast as the AD during that period of time, thus causing an excess demand in the market. The government increases prices of these goods/services in order to reduce its excess demand.

Demand-pull inflation (inflation caused due to excess demand) can be solved by increasing income taxes, which generally causes a decrease in demand due to people having less disposable income (amount of income left after subtracting taxes). Increase interest rates, when interest rates are high people tend to save more rather than consume, this is because the cost of borrowing money from banks becomes more expensive, therefore making 'saving' seems like a better option. The government should reduce spending, as mentioned in blog 23, one of the components that determines AD is 'government spending', this is because the government needs to collect resources for its projects, therefore it has to spend to buy the resources, so if government lowers its spending the AD will decrease.

Another cause which leads to higher inflation is; higher production cost for firms. When firms need to face higher production costs, they increase the price of their goods, in order to regain revenue. Higher production costs for firms can be due to higher cost of raw material, due to a rise in wages or buying more imports. When wages rise the firms need to give each worker a greater percentage of their revenue, therefore firms increase costs of goods in order to maintain profit. Firms might buy more imports, as the raw materials might be scarce in their country, and if the exchange rate is low, or there are high import tariffs (tax on trade), the cost of production will rise even drastically.

Solutions to solve 'cost-push inflation' (inflation caused due to higher production costs) include; try and strengthen the currency. As mentioned before a lower exchange rate will lead to import prices becoming dearer for the firms. If the exchange rate is bought up, the firms will face lower costs when buying imports. The government can provide subsidies (a sum of money provided by the government to help a firm/industry) to the firms, the firms therefore can use this extra money provided to buy their raw material or give wages. The government can work on improving productivity by firms, such as organising more training/education programs, in order for the workers to gain more knowledge/skills which can help them produce more. If more output is sold by the firms, the chances of gaining more profit (even at low prices) becomes higher.

Overall, these are the two causes and few solutions which can be carried out in order to solve inflation. These solutions may have some downsides, such as when the government spends money on organising training/education programs, they will need to invest on/in something, therefore AD increases, and this is undesirable for an economy that is already facing inflation. Despite this negative impact, if the education programs help workers in increase production, the firms will sell more output, therefore probably will keep lower prices, and also the AS of the economy will increase, meaning that possibly the AS is enough to satisfy the AD. This was just to tell that, although a solution may have short-term impacts, it can lead to long-term benefits.

Hope you all enjoyed!

ePrabhavnomics blog 27
Originally Published on: 10 March 2019

Types of unemployment in the economy

Unemployment is common in every economy, it is when, those in the working age (15-64 years) are unable to find work. Therefore it is calculated as a percentage of the population in working age group, that are out of work. As mentioned in one of my previous blogs (blog 24), one of the government's main objectives is to reach an unemployment rate of only 3% in the economy, since it is possible that there aren't enough jobs available to keep the unemployment rate at 0%. There are many different types (reasons) that cause unemployment in the economy. In this blog I will be explaining what the different types of unemployment are, and what causes them.

The first type of unemployment is 'cyclical unemployment'. The amount of economic growth at a certain period of time, decides whether this type of unemployment will occur. So, when the economy goes into recession (a period of negative economic growth), demand for goods/services usually drops, since incomes fall, firms therefore have more difficulty in gaining revenue, and are forced to lay-off workers in order to reduce costs. When the economy leaves recession, and experiences positive growth again, firms hire workers in order to satisfy the increased demand. The reason why this is called cyclical unemployment is because, there is an economic model named, 'the business cycle' which shows 'the natural rise and fall of economic growth that occurs over time.' The business cycle has 4 phases; boom (period of positive economic growth), downswing (falling economic growth), recession and upswing (recovery from recession). And this type of unemployment is influence by which phase of the business cycle the economy is currently at.

The next type is 'frictional unemployment'. Frictional unemployment is when, workers leave one job but still haven't found another job. Employees may want to find new jobs for higher salary or because their educational skills aren't being fully utilised in their old job, or even when workers are fired/laid-off. Frictional unemployment can also occur when those who have just finished their education are looking for work but unable to find it. This type of unemployment is inevitable, since anybody at any time can decide to leave their job. The economy might benefit from some frictional unemployment in the long-run, since if the workers get employed in a job where they can use their skills in a better way, they can become more efficient and this can help the economy grow. It is given this name because, when looking for a new job may workers need lots of time, and energy, similarly if an object has lots of friction it takes that object lots of time and energy in order to move.

Next is 'structural unemployment'. This type of unemployment occurs when either; an industry replaces humans with machinery to gain more efficiency/productivity, or an industry shuts down (usually due to huge revenue loss). In both the cases mentioned, the industry no longer requires any worker, and therefore this leads to those workers remaining unemployed, and these workers usually don't have the skills required for any other jobs. This unemployment is called in this way because, this unemployment occurs when the structure of the economy (a term that describes the output, trade, income and employment coming from the 3 sectors; primary (agricultural), secondary (machinery) and tertiary (services)) changes.

Last is 'seasonal unemployment'. Unemployment received by seasonal workers during the off-season. For example workers working in skiing resorts will face unemployment in summer since in that period demand for skiing dips, similarly those working in beaches will face unemployment during the winter months.

These are the different types of unemployment that can occur in the economy, in my next blog I will be talking about possible solutions to solve each of them. Hope you all enjoyed!

ePrabhavnomics blog 28

Originally Published on: 17 March 2019

Ways to solve unemployment

In my previous blog I wrote about different types of unemployment in the economy. In this blog I will be writing about possible ways to solve different types of unemployment. If you guys want some detail on what these different types of unemployments are, then please check out my previous blog (which is on my profile). Anyways, hope you enjoy!

The first type of unemployment we looked at was 'cyclical unemployment'. Explained briefly it is; when workers are laid-off by firms during recession (period of negative economic growth). The main cause of this employment is very little aggregate demand (AD- sum of demand for all goods/services in an economy at any given time) in the economy, the solution to solve this unemployment is to cause the AD in the economy to increase. The components which are taken into account while calculating AD are; Consumption by citizens + Investment by firms + Government Spending + (Exports- Imports). During a recession spending decreases, due to income/revenue declines. Solution could be, the government can increase investments, causing the AD to slightly increase, the government can also reduce taxation on incomes, for ease of spending. The banks can reduce interest rates for borrowing, this will make borrowing more attractive, since it is cheaper, and therefore will encourage expenditure by the consumers/firms. If the economy reduces its interest rates the currency will depreciate (go down), and therefore the number of exports will increase, as it will be cheaper to export.

The next is 'frictional unemployment'. Explained briefly it is; when a worker leaves a particular job and still hasn't found another one. It is difficult to control when someone decides to leave a particular job, and the job availability in the market also influences how easy it is to find a new job. One possible solution is, the firms can increase the wages of workers, and not underuse the highly skilled ones. If the workers are satisfied with their job the chances of them deciding to leave the job is minimal. If a person for any other reason decides to leave their job, for example change in city/country, they can search for different jobs before leaving, this way they probably won't have to face lots of time out of work.

Next is 'structural unemployment'. Explained briefly it is; when workers are replaced by machinery or when an industry shuts down, in short when a firm doesn't require workers anymore. This unemployment is mainly caused when the structure of the economy (a term that describes the output, trade, income and employment coming from the 3 sectors; primary (agricultural), secondary (machinery) and tertiary (services)) changes, when an economy develops it requires lesser workers in the primary sector and more in the tertiary one. The government can organise educational programs, to develop higher skills which can aid in getting a job easily. Same is when humans are replaced by machinery or an industry shuts down, in both these cases particular skills can prove as an upper-hand for workers when looking for another job. As a side note; when workers are in the educational programs they aren't considered unemployed, because they aren't actually looking for jobs during that period, only when looking for jobs and unable to find them, they are considered unemployed.

Lastly is 'seasonal unemployment'. Explained briefly it is; the unemployment faced by seasonal workers during the off-season, those working in skiing resorts in summer and those working by beaches in winter, in both these instances the people are unemployed, since demand for those places falls in those periods of the year. Possible solutions to solve this type of unemployment is the government can give these workers training, so that they can do another job in the off-season. The government can increase incomes of seasonal workers, to compensate their income for whole calendar year.

Overall, these were the possible solutions which can solve these 4 types of unemployment, hope you all enjoyed!

ePrabhavnomics blog 29
Originally Published on: 24 March 2019

Differences between the public sector and the private sector

Every economy is divided into two sectors: the public sector and the private sector. The public sector is the part of the economy that is owned and controlled by the government, and the private sector is the part of the economy that is run by private companies and organisations and not the government. Both of these sectors are completely different from each other, and in this blog I will be explaining these differences. In this blog I won't say which one I think is better, because I believe both are great in their own ways, it is up to you guys to decide which one is better. Hope you enjoy!

The first difference between them is; their aim. The public sector focuses on helping the citizens and fulfilling their demands, the private sector on the other hand has the goal of creating new markets (make new goods/services) in order to make profit. The private sector firms should always answer stakeholders (person, group or organisation which has interest in a business) and customers, what this means is that, the private sector firms must make sure they satisfy consumer demands. Even if the public sector is inefficient, they can still stay in business, meanwhile in the private sector if firms are poorly run they will go out of business. This is because, every country only has one government, meanwhile there are many industries in the private sector, and the businesses in the private sector have to face lots of competition. You might note that both have to accomplish demands of consumers, but the difference is, the public sector does this to make developments in the country, while the private sector does this to increase its revenue.

The next difference between them is; the way they earn money. The private sector makes money from selling its goods/services, while the public sector earns money from taxes.

Next difference is; how employees are hired. Usually it takes shorter for you to get a job in the private sector, when compared to the public sector. The reason for this is because, when the economy goes out of recession (a period of negative economic growth), and re-enters positive economic growth (boom), the demand for the goods/services grows and to meet the demand firms need more workers, in order to produce more and gain more revenue, and the opposite when the economy enters recession, this is also called, 'cyclical unemployment' (read blog 27 to know more about this). Therefore when the economy is in the boom phase, the chances of being employed in a private sector job is higher. Meanwhile in the public sector, it could also take years to get a job, because a new position has to be created for the employee applying, which is a long process.

Not just hiring process, but also the benefits of working are different for both sectors. In the private sector, you can expect a better salary, and more incentives to improve your productivity and quality, due to higher competition. Meanwhile in the public sector, you have a higher job security (having a job that you are unlikely to be dismissed from), retirement benefits, higher allowances (an amount of money paid habitually to someone to meet their needs/expenses), and perquisites (a benefit which one is granted due to their job/position).

Last difference is; how employees are promoted. In the public sector, employees are promoted by 'Seniority', this means that when an employee has been part of the job for longer, they will reach a higher position. Meanwhile in the private sector, performance of employees leads to their promotion.

These are some of the important differences between these two sectors, As said in the introduction, I will not decide which of these two sectors is better, and I will leave it up to you all to decide. Anyways, hope you liked it! Thanks for reading.

ePrabhavnomics blog 30
Originally Published on: 31 March 2019

Impacts of Brexit on UK's economy

Brexit is defined as, 'UK's withdrawal from the European Union (EU). Britain+Exit=Brexit. The UK was expected to leave the EU on 29 March 2019, however since the UK hasn't yet accepted the 'Brexit Withdrawal Agreement', (an agreement between the UK and the EU on how to implement Brexit) this date has gotten delayed to 12 April. Brexit is going to cause lots of negative economic impacts for the UK. This blog is going to explain the economic impacts which the UK will face post Brexit.

Firstly exporting will be dearer. UK being a member of the EU, benefits from free trade (being able to trade goods/services without any restrictions, for example taxes) across other EU countries. There are also many non-EU members which the EU has made trade agreements with, this means the EU members can also benefit from free trade to those countries. After the UK leaves, the UK may face tariffs (import/export taxes) while trading to other EU and non-EU members, and will have to make trade agreements with frequent traders in order to benefit from free trade.

The UK is expected to grow slowly when outside the EU. Post-Brexit the economy of the UK will grow at slower rates constantly, and this will therefore lead to a decline in incomes. A major reason for the UK's expected sluggish economic growth is due to lower investment by firms. The companies will be insecure about the future and therefore would prefer to save then invest, therefore will cause the amount of output produced by the UK to sharply decline. Consumers will also save more rather than spend due to high uncertainty about the future.

Lower employment rate. If firms decide to cut investment, their chances of increasing revenue declines, when companies have limited revenue, they will have to lay-off workers or else they will face financial crisis, since they will have to give workers their pay. Unemployment rates will rise due to this, until the economy gets back in the boom phase (period of rapid economic growth), these workers will remain unemployed.

Inflation spikes. Inflation in the UK is expected to be twice as high as it was pre-Brexit. Inflation raises the cost of living in the country, and since the incomes are rising at a slower rate compared to the rate at which prices rise, purchasing power in the UK will dip. Rise in prices of goods/services also decreases the chances of foreign firms buying UK exports, therefore making UK goods seem less competitive worldwide.

The pound is becoming weaker. A weaker pound will be a problem for those living inside the UK, since when going abroad they will have to pay more, however for those coming to the UK this will be advantage, since they will find it cheaper to enter the UK. Exports from the UK will be cheaper, yes there is inflation going on, but still a weaker pound will make UK goods seem cheaper for foreign companies. If exports from the UK rise, there is hope that the UK firms will be incentivised to increase production, and this could help revive the British economy.

Overall, this is how the British economy will be impacted if Brexit takes place. Most of these consequences are negative, however as stated in the end the economy could revive if exports are increased, but still demand for UK exports may not increase necessarily. Everything is uncertain, we will have to wait in order to know what will happen.

Hope you enjoyed! Thanks for reading!

ePrabhavnomics blog 31

Originally Published on: 7 April 2019

Impacts on EU due to Brexit

Last week I wrote about the economic impacts the UK will face due to Brexit, and we saw that they were mostly negative. However, how will the EU get impacted by Brexit? This blog will be exploring the consequences the EU will face after Brexit. Before starting; if any of you is interested in reading my previous blog, you can find it on my profile. As a side note; if the relationship between the UK and the EU remains amicable post-Brexit the impact of these consequences might be reduced.

Firstly, the EU's total GDP (total goods and services produced by an economy annually), will drop after UK's exit. UK has the 2nd highest GDP in the EU (after Germany). The sum of all EU countries' GDP with UK is US$20.9 trillion, and without the UK it is US$18.28 trillion. This means that the EU will be producing less output, and therefore fewer foreign firms will make trades with the EU. In fact, the UK is the largest EU exporter (to non-

EU countries), responsible for 22% of EU's International exports. Therefore we can say that the EU will face huge export losses due to Brexit. The UK might be producing goods which other countries in the EU might not be producing/producing fewer of, if the EU is in dire need of goods, they will have to make a trade-agreement (a formal agreement made between 2 or more countries about improving trade with each other) with the UK in order to benefit from free trade (being able to trade without facing any restrictions, such as taxes). In this case, not only EU members, but the UK will also have to make such trade agreements with other non-EU, frequent traders.

The EU's total budget will also reduce post-Brexit. The UK contributes to 11.82% of the EU's budget, and it is on 4th place (after Germany, France and Italy). This means that the EU will have lower funds to distribute to its members. The poorer members will be most affected by the EU's lower budget, since they will need the most funding and the EU may not be able to provide them with those funds.

The UK has been an important figure for the EU when it came to foreign affairs and defence, since the UK has one of the EU's strongest military, and many other strengths which other countries lack. Without the UK, the EU's foreign policy (a government strategy in dealing with other nations) may be less influential, the EU may be exposed to greater external threats. In short, the EU will have lost a key asset, and therefore their international relations may be at stake.

The type of laws made in the European Parliament might be different. The UK has the 3rd highest number of seats in the European Parliament (73 seats), after Germany (96 seats), France (74 seats). These 73 seats will be given to other countries, but they will have different thoughts when compared to the UK people, therefore the law in the EU might be different post-Brexit. I am not saying that the laws passed by the Parliament without the UK will be bad, I am just saying they will be different, and this could possibly have an effect on the EU citizens, since they won't be acquainted with these differences.

Overall, UK's exit from the EU will be detrimental both for UK itself, and the EU. It can also be seen that most of the public is now against Brexit, and Brexit is also getting constantly delayed. Therefore let's just hope it never happens, so that the future will be positive.

Thanks for reading!

ePrabhavnomics blog 32
Originally Published on: 14 April 2019

Negative impacts of economic growth

Economic growth is important for every economy, since it helps to increase people's incomes, meaning they have a better standard of living, and economic growth is a sign of greater output (goods and services) coming out of the economy. However, economic growth doesn't only bring positive effects, there are also some negative impacts economic growth can have on the economy. Firstly, before starting I would like to point out that the ideal rate of economic growth is between 2% and 3% per annum, when economic growth exceeds 4% the consequences which I will be explaining in this blog are most likely to be faced by the economy, remember; 'anything in excess is bad'.

Likely environmental damage. Usually consumption rises when the economy grows, therefore it is possible that demand for air travel increases, similarly the number of vehicles on the street will also increase, since the citizens have greater income to spend. In both these cases, air pollution will increase, and will affect the health of the citizens. On the other hand firms may be incentivised to produce more (since more consumers are buying their goods), and this extra production might cause the factories to emit more carbon emissions, again increasing air pollution in the area, possibly the firms may dump their waste in water bodies nearby and therefore also increase water pollution. Similarly, if new firms enter the market/or a current firm decides to expand, they will need space to set up their factory, and this might mean they will have to cut down trees in order to acquire land, this means the greenery in the economy is reducing.

Inflation likely to rise. As mentioned in the introduction; economic growth leads to higher incomes, therefore consumption is also likely to rise. If aggregate demand (AD- sum of demand for all goods/services in an economy during a period of time), rises faster than aggregate supply (AS- total supply of goods/services in an economy during a period of time), the price will rise in order to try and reduce some of the greater AD. Similarly, if firms have a greater revenue (due to higher AD) they may invest more money in projects, therefore they will have to increase prices of goods, in order to regain their high budget. This also leads to inflation.

Resource depletion. If firms decide to extract more natural resources for their projects, in the longer run the economy will see a decline in these resources, possibly also an end to them. This will impact the future generation, since they won't be able to benefit from these resources which we currently are able to. These resources may be important for a country to help their economy grow (since these countries can export these resources to other countries that need them, but don't have them), for example oil in Saudi Arabia or petroleum in most of North Africa.

Income inequality will rise. The benefits of the growth may not be evenly spread across the country. This is because the benefiters is dependent on those who are driving the growth, for example, if an economy is more 'agricultural-based', those who work in the agriculture industry will gain the most profit. The economy which will be most impacted is, the one were the rich people are driving the growth, as in that country the poor won't be able to enjoy greater income since they aren't working in the industry which is leading the growth. And, the gap between the rich and the poor will increase in that country.

Overall, it can be seen that economic growth does have some very harmful consequences, and therefore the economy should try and restrict growth to 3% annually. The economy can also try and minimise the consequences of these impacts, for example; the government can place a tax on industries for emitting excess greenhouse gases. The government can also place taxes on the extra income. The government can also give subsidies (a financial aid to businesses), to help businesses which are currently producing a small amount of output, to increase their production, thus helping them increase their share of growth benefit.

Thanks for reading! Hope you all enjoyed!

ePrabhavnomics blog 33
Originally Published on: 21 April 2019

Differences between Republic and Monarchy

A country is either a republic or a monarchy. A republic country is a country which is ruled by the government (most of the countries in the world are republics), and a monarch country is a country which is ruled by the King/Queen (examples; United Kingdom, Malaysia, United Arab Emirates). There are many differences between these two different forms of government. In this blog I will be explaining these differences. Hope you all enjoy!

Before starting I would like to wish a Happy 93rd Birthday to UK's longest ruling Queen (67 years of ruling), Queen Elizabeth II.

Before coming to my first difference, I would also like to point out one thing, a monarchy can be divided into two categories; a constitutional monarchy and an absolute monarchy. A constitutional monarchy is when the country does have a king/queen however the country also has a government (eg, United Kingdom), in these cases the power of the king/queen is limited by the government, however the government has to take permission from the king/queen when making decisions. Meanwhile in an absolute monarchy the king/queen has unlimited power (eg, Saudi Arabia). The blog will be talking about absolute monarchies.

Firstly, the voting system. In a republic, the citizens chose who they want as their head of state (prime minister/president), with the population casting a vote and then the candidate that gets the majority of votes becomes head of state. Meanwhile in a monarchy, the children of the current rulers will become the new ones, meaning that the king's son will become the new king after the current king passes away. Also the term (period of time the head of state stays in office) is different in both these forms of government, so in a republic the new head of state is elected every 5 years, while in a monarchy the ruler will change only when the current one dies or abdicates (resigns from the throne- plus the King of Japan will be abdicating on 30 April), and this can take several decades. In a monarchy the change of ruler is less violent when compared to a republic, since the new ruler is already known by the public, in a republic when electing the new head of state there may be many protests.

Competency of the head of state. In a republic the head of state themselves chose to become the head of state, meaning they decide to candidate themselves for the election, and are more likely to become competent rulers. Meanwhile in a monarchy the new ruler is the child of the current ruler, and so they are forced to take that position of, they may not want to take these huge responsibilities, or aren't proficient enough to rule, this could be a weak point for the country. Also, in a republic the head of state needs to be over 18 to rule, meanwhile in a monarchy there is no age barrier, which is another disadvantage, as someone at a young age may be unable to rule efficiently.

Next is, ease of passing law. Usually in a monarchy passing laws is easier when compared to a republic. This is because, monarchies have one ruler, they have unlimited power, therefore they can pass law without facing any opposition. Conversely, in a republic the new law goes to parliament, and then there is a debate on it, followed by a vote on whether to pass it or not. This can be positive for a monarchy if the new law has favourable impacts on the society, but also negative, since the new law could be unhelpful to the society and no-one is able to oppose it, meanwhile in the republic the law will be passed only if it is beneficial. Also in a republic the public is able to protest against a law which they disagree with.

Taxes rates. Monarchies have high tax rates when compared to republics. The workers in a monarchy have to provide the costs that the ruler requires during its office term. Republics may also have high tax rates, but still the government has other methods to get revenue (eg, loans). Also the workers in a republic doesn't have to pay the costs faced by the head of state in their personal life, which in a monarchy the citizens have to do (pay the costs faced the king/queen in their personal life).

Overall, both these forms of government are very different from each other, and they both have their own advantages/disadvantages. I won't come to a conclusion of 'which one is better', I will leave that with you guys to decide. And I am not trying to dishonour either of them by stating their disadvantages, I am just stating their differences.

Hope you enjoyed! Thanks for reading!

ePrabhavnomics blog 34

Originally Published on: 28 April 2019

How does economic development and happiness of a country correlate?

It is assumed that, if a country has greater economic development, that country's people are happier, this is because higher economic development means better lifestyle among the citizens. However, is this really the case? Does more economic development really mean more happiness? Well, in this blog I will be analysing if greater economic development means more happiness in the world. Hope you enjoy!

Just as a recap, economic development consists of a country becoming; wealthier, healthier and having better access to education. A country needs all 3 of these to become economically developed. To see how 'happy' a country is, I will be using the 'World Happiness Report'. Which is a ranking published every year by the United Nations (UN) to show how happy each country is. A sample of citizens (around 1000) in every country are asked how happy they are, from 0-10 (10 being happiest), and then the UN, using the scores told by the citizens, formulates a number from 0-10, which represents how happy the country is.

Lets start by seeing which country is ranked top in the individual factors required by a country, in order to be economically developed; Japan has the highest life expectancy, which is 'number of years a person can expect to live'. Also Japan has the lowest infant mortality rate, which is, 'number of infants that die before turning 1 year old, out of 1000 live births'. This shows us that Japan is the healthiest country in the world.

Qatar has the highest GDP per capita, which is the 'total GDP of a country (total good and services produced in a year), divided by the total population'. This means that Qatar is the wealthiest in the world.

Meanwhile the country with the highest education is; Australia. It has the highest education index. The education index takes into account; expected years of schooling (number of years in school a child can expect to receive), and combines average number of years of eduction which someone aged above 25 years has received in his lifetime. The mean of these two gives the education index.

The 3 countries mentioned above were the ones which were ranked at the top for each individual component. The country which is ranked at the top after combining all of these 3 components is; Norway.

Now that you know which country is faring the best in each of the components, let's look at where these 4 countries are ranked on the 'World Happiness Report 2018'. There are a total of 156 countries in this ranking. Japan is ranked on number 54, Qatar is ranked on 32, Australia is on 10, and Norway is on 2. None of these ranks are bad, however Japan and Qatar are ranked lower than many countries, who have performed much worse then them in the components in which they were ranked first. For example, countries like Brazil (ranked 28) and Argentina (ranked 29), whose GDP per capita, and life expectancy is much lower than that of Qatar and Japan, are ranked above these two countries.

Overall, we can see that there is no real correlation between economic development and happiness. Although the top countries on the happiness index are very economically developed, while the bottom ones on the happiness index are very less economically developed, in the middle of the ranking, the countries' ranks doesn't show their economic development. Possible reasons for this include; the richer the country, the workers have more pressure to improve production of output, therefore stress levels are higher in richer countries. Meanwhile, in healthier countries, there are more elderly people, and since they have nothing to do, they might feel bored and unhappy. Also, happiness is subjective, everyone has a different definition of happiness, and it is difficult for one to measure how happy they are. This is also a possible reason why some countries might have gotten lower/higher rankings. Anyways, hope you liked the blog!

ePrabhavnomics blog 35
Originally Published on: 5 May 2019

Advantages and Disadvantages of a Monopoly for consumers

Usually there are many firms that sell a particular product to the consumers, however there are times when a particular product is only sold by one firm. In these cases the firm is a monopoly. The definition of a monopoly is; 'an organisation or group that has complete control over something (the consumers in this case), especially an area of business, so that others have no share'. There are many differences between having a monopoly, and having many different firms selling the same product, and these differences do affect consumers, in a positive and negative way. This blog will explain how having a monopoly can be an advantage for the consumers and how it can be a disadvantage at the same time. Hope you all enjoy!

Starting with the advantages; a monopoly is able to research and develop their products according to consumer needs. Since a monopoly's revenue is higher compared to the revenue in perfect competition (opposite of monopoly – many firms selling the same product), the monopoly is able to use its extra revenue to develop their product. The consumers therefore are able to benefit from these better products.

A monopoly is able to afford latest technology, for the same reason as the previous paragraph (higher revenue), the monopoly can use the latest technology for producing their goods. Due to this, they might end up producing greater output, and consumers will benefit from this (especially if the good has huge demand), since they can purchase more of that good. This also helps increase a monopoly's efficiency.

A monopoly is able to benefit from economies of scale; economies of scale is defined as, 'long run falling average costs'. This means that as, time passes and the monopoly becomes more efficient, it can reduce the cost of its good and at the same time produce/sell greater output. In perfect competition firms are unable to benefit from economies of scale because, a firm is unable to produce large output of that good, since their revenue is limited. Economies of scale benefits the consumers by giving them the opportunity to consume more at a lower cost.

Now let's start with the disadvantages; higher prices. Since a monopoly is the only firm selling that particular product, they can raise their prices, and unfortunately, the consumers will be forced to continue buying the goods from that firm. In a perfect competition, if a firm does this (raises its prices), they will go out of business, since the consumers can easily start buying goods from another firm.

Apart from, charging higher prices, the monopoly might sell products of low quality. The same reason as the previous paragraph is applicable here. I did mention in the advantages that a monopoly might use its extra revenue to develop its product, but still it can be lazy and produce goods of poor quality, and the monopoly won't risk running out of business, especially if the product has high demand. Raising prices and producing low quality goods can be referred to as 'consumer exploitation'.

Overall, these are some advantages and disadvantages of having a monopoly market. I will leave it up to you guys to decide whether a monopoly overall is advantage or a disadvantages for consumers. Also before concluding I would like to point out that; a new firm can also start selling that same good as a current monopoly is in order to give the current monopoly some competition, however it will take a long time for the new firm to become big enough to compete with the current monopoly, especially if the current monopoly doesn't do something mentioned in the disadvantages, and only does the things mentioned in the advantages.

ePrabhavnomics blog 36

Originally Published on: 12 May 2019

Advantages and Disadvantages of Perfect Competition for consumers

Last week I wrote a blog about the benefits and costs faced by consumers in a monopoly market. For those who don't remember, a monopoly is defined as, 'an organisation or group that has complete control over something (the consumers in this case), especially an area of business, so that others have no share'. Which in short means, when a particular good is sold by only one firm. This blog will be exploring how perfect competition (opposite of monopoly – many firms selling the same product) can be good and bad for the consumers. Hope you enjoy!

Let's start with the advantages; chances of consumer exploitation is very low. Consumer exploitation is when the producers take advantage of the buyers, for example they increase prices or decrease quality of the good. If a firm in perfect competition does either of the two, they will go out of business, because the consumers will easily be able to switch to another company. In a monopoly a firm doesn't risk anything by using this strategy (consumer exploitation), because they are the only sellers of that product, and consumers will be forced to buy only from them. In conclusion, the consumers will never face either problem (high prices and/or low quality) when buying from a firm in perfect competition.

Now let's start with the disadvantages; due to limited revenue the firms can't develop their product. Since there are many firms competing with each other (by selling the same product), no firm is able to receive huge amounts of profit, due to this the companies are unable to innovate and develop their good, and consumers will be forced to buy ordinary products from the firms. Due to lack of product development, it is possible that the good purchased by consumers are of inferior quality, there are few sectors in which this could prove to be detrimental for the consumers, for example, food sector, medicine sector.

Limited choice; this might come as a surprise to many of you, since you might be thinking that, 'if many firms are selling the same good, how is it possible that consumers have a restricted choice?' The answer is that; the product sold by every firm is homogenous, meaning that, it is identical, there is no difference in the products. This point to some extent links to my previous point, finite revenue due to which firms can't develop their good. In perfect competition the firms try and 'copy' the products sold by others, because since they can easily go out of business, selling goods of inferior quality is not prudent for them. Comparing this with a monopoly, although only one firm sells that good, they have ample revenue, which they can use to develop their product.

A firm is unable to benefit from economies of scale, this means, 'long run falling average costs', this means that, as a firm produces extra output, it can reduce its prices. Consumers can hugely benefit from this, as they are able to buy extra output for a lower cost. Unfortunately, in perfect competition this isn't possible, since limited revenue leads to an unlikely chance to increase output. And, if one of the firms reduces its prices, then every other firm will do so too. So overall, a single firm in perfect competition can't benefit from economies of scale, because every other firm will 'copy' what one firm does.

Overall, this is how perfect competition can benefit consumers, as well as prove to be harmful for them. You might also have noticed that the advantages of a monopoly are the disadvantages here, meanwhile the advantages here are the disadvantages of a monopoly. Overall, I believe a monopoly is slightly better than perfect competition, due to the fact that a monopoly has greater revenue to develop its product, and can benefit from economies of scale, a monopoly should also avoid consumer exploitation. Hope you enjoyed! As a side note; there are more market structures, not just 'monopoly' and 'perfect competition'. I will be explaining them in my future blogs.

ePrabhavnomics blog 37
Originally Published on: 19 May 2019

Advantages and Disadvantages of an Oligopoly for Consumers

The last two blogs were on two different types of market structures; monopolies and perfect competition. This blog will also be on a market structure, which is an 'oligopoly'. An oligopoly is defined as, 'a market form with limited competition in which a few producers control the majority of the market share and typically produce similar products'. This blog will be explaining how an oligopoly can be beneficial as well as disadvantageous for the consumers. Hope you enjoy!

Before starting I would like to point out how an oligopoly is different from perfect competition. So, in perfect competition, there are many firms selling a particular product and there are low barriers to entry, barriers to entry is defined as, 'obstacles, such as start-up costs (the cost to start a business) that stops a new firm from entering the market'. In an oligopoly the barriers to entry are high, and the number of firms in the market is comparatively lower.

Let's start with the advantages; competition might be present. As mentioned in the definition, in an oligopoly there are two or more firms selling the same product, therefore competition is still possible in an oligopoly. Competition forces firms to produce goods of high quality and set lower prices because consumer exploitation (high prices or low-quality goods) will lead to firms running out of business, as the consumers can easily switch to another firm. Consumers will therefore, be able to benefit from lower prices and better products.

Higher revenue can be used to develop and innovate the product. As in an oligopoly, there are few firms selling the product, the firms are still able to receive reasonably high profits, these high profits can be used to improve their products, and suit consumers needs in a better way. This is something which lacks in perfect competition since the firms are unable to earn a great amount of profit, which is due to a greater number of companies in the market.

Now onto the disadvantages; collusion is possible, which will reduce competition. In an oligopoly firms can 'collude' which means working together. When two or more firms collude, they become a sort of monopoly. When this happens the firms can use 'consumer exploitation' as a means to increase their revenue. The effect of this will depend on, how many firms have decided to collude, if all firms in the oligopoly have decided to collude, the consumers won't be able to switch to other firms and will have to face high prices. If only a few of the firms have decided to collude, consumers still have a choice to switch to another seller.

Limited choice; if firms are competitive, they may sell homogenous (identical) products, this restricts consumers from buying a variety of the same good. Although the companies are able to develop the product they sell, the other sellers may 'copy' every step made the company, again leading to consumers not receiving a diversity of the same good. This is very similar to perfect competition, in which firms are forced to be competitive, however, in an oligopoly being competitive is optional. In a monopoly meanwhile, although only one producer is selling those goods, as that producer doesn't have the threat of running out of business, the producer can still sell the same good in several varieties.

Overall, these are some of the advantages and disadvantages of an oligopoly. Some may have noticed that an oligopoly has the characteristics of both a monopoly and of perfect competition however it is less extreme when compared to both of them. Overall I believe that an oligopoly is better than a monopoly and perfect competition because it can benefit from better product development and lower chance of consumer exploitation, the other two market structures aren't able to benefit from both of them. If the oligopoly doesn't do as mentioned in the disadvantages, the consumers can receive high satisfaction.

Thanks for reading! Hope you enjoyed!

ePrabhavnomics blog 38
Originally Published on: 26 May 2019

How has India changed since 2014?

One 23 May 2019 the result of India's general elections was announced. The winner, as many of you may know was, the BJP (Bharatiya Janata Party), which won by a significant amount, by acquiring 303 seats in Parliament, and the political party at 2nd place (INC – Indian National Congress) only had 52 seats. The BJP has been ruling India since 2014, and has helped the country make significant progress. This blog will be looking at how India has changed since 2014 to the present day. Hope you all enjoy! PS: This blog will be focusing only on the positives.

The 'Make In India' initiative had been launched (in 2014). This initiative was launched in order to encourage companies to produce their products in India, and increase investment in manufacturing. It had an aim of creating jobs and enhancing skills, in 25 sectors of the economy (such as; automobiles, biotechnology, electrical machinery). This initiative also wanted to transform India into a global hub for design and production. As a result of this initiative India received greater foreign investment, a total of US$60.1 billion foreign investment in 2016, which is higher than that of China and USA. Apart from this, India's rank in the 'Ease of doing business index' (how easy it is to do a business in a country) increased. Also its rank on the 'Global Competitiveness Index' (assesses a country's ability to provide their citizens with high levels of prosperity) also improved. In conclusion, the country had; more jobs, more foreign investment and better rank in many prosperity indexes.

There has been significant improvement in quality of rural people. Examples of improvement include; increased number of housing in the country (18.22 lakhs in 2014 to 65 lakhs in 2019), similarly the government successfully provided rural households with access to clean sanitation (40% of total population had access to sanitation in 2014, now in 2019 it is 90% which has access to sanitation). Also, percentage of households with electricity connections have hugely increased, in January 2019 96% of households across the country had access to electricity.

The Goods and Services Tax (GST), which was launched in 2017. This is an indirect tax (a tax added to goods/services). This indirect tax replaced all the past indirect taxes, and now rather than several indirect taxes, there is only one (which is the GST). This tax has many advantages for consumers, for example, consumers don't have to face many indirect taxes so can benefit from lower prices,

Although this scheme wasn't completely successful I decided to add this, because it was a courageous attempt. I am talking about the '2016 banknote demonetisation'. This involved the 500 and

1000 rupee notes being banned, which forced people to got to banks and exchange their old notes with the new ones. This scheme was launched in order to eradicate black money from the economy. This scheme wasn't a complete success, since still around 107.2 billion rupees weren't deposited to the banks, although a much greater amount (15.3 trillion rupees) were deposited. This move also reduced the country's GDP (gross domestic product – total goods and services produced by a country annually) growth rate and industrial production.

Overall, these are some of the areas in which the BJP has helped India progress over the past 5 years. Although they weren't perfect, and brought only positive effects to the country, it is safe to say most of the schemes they carried out were beneficial. Therefore we can expect India to progress rapidly until the next general elections (which will be in 2024). Let's hope for the best! Anyways, thanks for reading my blog! Hope you liked it!

Good luck to Narendra Modi.

ePrabhavnomics blog 39
Originally Published on: 2 June 2019

Major International Organisations and their roles

This world has many international organisations, which look at many different issues/subjects taking place in the world. Every country is able to become a member of any international organisation, which if they do, then that international organisation will help that country, in achieving that organisation's goal. The exact definition of an international organisation is, 'an organisation with an International membership, scope or presence'. In this blog, I will be looking at few major international organisation and their roles. So hope you enjoy!

PS: I am not including the United Nations (UN) because, it has many different organisations within it and I will only be focusing on single organisations, however few of the organisations within the UN will be mentioned in this blog. Also, I already have a separate blog dedicated to the UN (blog 13). So let's get started.

The first one I will be talking about is the; World Health Organisation (WHO). This is an organisation within the UN, and it's role is 'to make sure everyone in the world has the highest possible level of health'. The WHO aims to accomplish this goal is by; help government in strengthening health care services, to work towards eradicating many diseases, to work with specialised agencies in order to improve: nutrition, housing, sanitation, hygiene and to work with other specialised organisations in order to prevent injuries. This organisation studies; spread of diseases (communicable and non-communicable), environmental health (pollution, UV radiation) lifestyle.

The World Bank. This isn't part of the UN, and it provides loans to countries where industrial projects are underway. The World Bank recently declared that its goal is to reduce poverty. The World Bank worked with the government of many LEDCs (less economically developed countries) in order to help reduce poverty, with the governments telling the World Bank the country's targets and priorities. The World Bank has also funded countries in order to help them adapt to climate change, and to help countries improve food security (state of having access to sufficient quantity of affordable, nutritious food).

World Trade Organisation (WTO). This organisation deals with trade regulation, provides a framework for negotiating trade agreements, settles trade disputes, and it operates via a system of trade rules. Usually, governments go to the WTO when trying to sort out trade problems faced with each other. When solving trade problems the WTO makes sure to be; not favour one nation over another, lower cost of trading, make trading safe (not affect the environment and health of public/animals).

Food and Agriculture Organisation of the United Nations. This organisation as from the name is part of the UN, and its purpose is to defeat hunger. This organisation aids LEDCs to improve practices in agriculture, forestry, and fisheries, and it also ensures good nutrition and food security. This organisation has launched several programs in order to solve these issues. For example the

'TeleFood campaign' in 1997, this campaign involved concerts, sporting events and many other activities which worked towards raising awareness about the issues of hunger. This campaign earned around US$28 million in donations. This money helped pay for small-scale farmers to increase food production.

In conclusion, these are few international organisation which are important in helping the world improve in becoming sustainable for the future. There are many more international organisations in this world, however, I believe these are a few of the most important ones. If you want to know about the ones which I didn't include in the blog, then let me know in the comment section below.

Hope you enjoyed!

<u>ePrabhavnomics blog 40</u>
Originally Published on: 9 June 2019

Major International Organisations and their roles (2)

Last week I wrote a blog on 'Major International Organisations and their roles'. An international organisation can be defined as, 'an organisation with an International membership, scope or presence'. If you can remember from last week, the list wasn't complete I was just listing down the ones I felt were the most important. In this blog I will be continuing/finishing the list. Hope you all enjoy!

The first one I will be talking about is; the World Labour Organisation (ILO). This is an organisation within the UN, and has an aim of promoting social justice and encourage decent work by setting International labour standards. The International labour standards developed by the ILO are aimed at stimulating opportunities for both genders in obtaining; satisfactory and productive work, within free, equal and safe conditions. The ILO has access to labour statistics of over 200 countries, which includes information on; employment, wages, economic growth, due to this the ILO is able to see which areas of the world needs most improvement and their attention. Over the past few years the ILO has tried to fight against many issues around the world like; forced labour (when people are forced to do a certain job), minimum wage law (a law due to which workers cannot be paid below a certain amount at an hourly/weekly/yearly rate) and child labour.

Next we have; World Tourism Organisation (UNWTO). This is an organisation within the UN, and has an aim to promote responsible, sustainable and universally accessible tourism. With this aim it hopes to achieve; economic development, peace, human rights, freedom for all. Tourism policies (a public policy, which comprises of different objectives related to tourism) are made in this organisation. This organisation encourages the usage of the 'Global Code of Ethics for Tourism' (a set of principles made to promote tourism development). The Global Code of Ethics for Tourism will help increase contribution of tourism to economic development, and reduce the negative effects.

Next on the list we have; United Nations Educational, Scientific and Cultural Organisation (UNESCO). It's roles is to contribute to peace and security by encouraging international collaboration in education, sciences and culture, in order to raise universal respect for justice, human rights and law. It aims to achieve its goals by conducting 5 major programs; education, natural sciences, social/human sciences, culture and communication/information. The projects which it has sponsored include; teacher-training programs, international science programs, promoting independent media and freedom of the press, regional and cultural history projects.

Last we have; United Nations Human Settlements Programme (UN-Habitat). It has the goal of promoting socially and environmentally sustainable cities and towns, it also is responsible for providing adequate shelter to all. This organisation work in over 70 countries across 5 continents and focus on these following areas; urban planning and design, urban economy, urban basic services, housing and slum upgrading, reducing risk, rehabilitation. The UN-Habitat has worked with the governments of many 'less economically developed countries' (LEDCs) in order to build more settlements within those countries.

Overall, these were few of the major international organisations and their aims. They are in no particular order, and although I missed some, I believe these are the most important ones. Hope you all liked this blog! Thanks for reading! Which ones do you guys think are the most important? Let me know in the comments section!

ePrabhavnomics blog 41
Originally Published on: 16 June 2019

Free Trade and its impacts

Trading goods and services is a common practice between countries, done especially because the country of destination is unable to produce what the country of origin is and allows consumers to be open to more and possibly diverse products. For example an American consumer can decide whether to buy an American, Japanese or French car. Sometimes trade can be restricted by the importing country placing tariffs (trade taxes to be paid when importing/exporting). An import quota (another trade restriction) can also be placed, which restricts the physical quantity of a good which can be imported in a country, over a period of time. However, a trade can also face no restrictions, and this is known as 'free trade'. This blog will be explaining free trade and whether it is beneficial or not.

Free trade like anything has both advantages and disadvantages, so let's begin with the advantages. Gives wider option to consumers and at lower prices. Since the goods can be imported from any country, without any restrictions, the consumers are able to choose between variety of different goods. Apart from just consumers, it can also benefit the country, since the country will be able to purchase goods which they are unable to produce. The lack of restrictions allow the country of destination to benefit from lower prices.

Leads to economic growth. When more foreign demand for a particular countries' goods increases, the countries' aggregate demand (AD) rises, since exports increase (to know more about AD look at my blog 23). Although the price of the goods many be low, if the overall number of exports increase, the revenue received by exporting firms may see a rise, which will lead to economic growth. More jobs can be created in the domestic market, since firms may need more workers, in order to increase production of goods, which will be later exported to foreign countries. Apart from just the exporting country, even the importing country can see economic growth due to free trade, because the importing country sees an increase in resources, which can be used for improving their countries' production.

Competition allows countries to be more efficient. Many countries can be competing to sell the same good. Competition forces countries to improve the quality of their good, or lower price. This leads to nations benefitting from better quality goods. This benefits both the importing and exporting country. Importing country receives better quality goods and exporting country is able to export more output (due to lower prices).

Now that the advantages are done, let's start with the disadvantages. Environmental damage. Whether the goods come by ship or airplane be pollution will be caused, regardless of trading quantity. Since trading will increase, due to no restrictions, concentrations of pollution in the air and water will both increase.

Less use of domestic goods. If a country imports excess amount of foreign goods, the goods produced by local sellers will face lower demand, and this will cause the economy's AD to fall. A falling AD will lead to the economy's growth to slow or even become negative. Unemployment might also increase, because when demand for a firms' goods falls, they lay-off workers, in order to reduce their production costs (worker's wages).

Pressure on exporting countries. If demand for a country's goods drastically rises, the country may be under pressure in order to produce high amounts of that good. This may result in workers working for extra hours, and in stressful conditions. If exporting country is a 'less economically developed country' (LEDCs), workers may not receive the extra pay.

Overall these were few of the advantages and disadvantages of free trade. I believe it is beneficial for all countries, however it should be used in limit only. If you look, you will notice all the disadvantages are due to countries demanding excess foreign exports. So, a country shouldn't start importing goods non-stop. Hope you all enjoyed! Thanks for reading!

<u>**ePrabhavnomics blog 42**</u>
Originally Published on: 23 June 2019

Effects of a balance of payments deficit for an economy

Trading is good for a country's economy, and for this reasons every country trades their goods with other countries. The quantity of imports and exports for every country are different, due to the country's different needs. The difference between the exports and imports is shown by the country's 'balance of payments' (BoP). The BoP shows the value of money received from exports minis money spent on imports. If an economy has more exports that imports, it is said the economy has a 'balance of payments surplus'. If the opposite is true (more imports than exports), the economy has a 'balance of payments deficit'. This blog will be looking at whether a BoP deficit is really a drawback for an economy.

Let's start with the negative impacts of a BoP deficit. Unemployment in the country, or workers face low wages. Since firms are spending more than they are receiving, they will have limited capital left, and will be more willing to save than spend (unless absolutely necessary). Therefore, possibly they may lay-off workers, thus causing unemployment to rise, even if the workers aren't laid-off, they may be subject to low wages. Also, it is possible that, if demand for imports is high, demand for locals goods might fall, and local workers' utility may fall.

Firms might have to borrow from foreign countries in order to buy imports. If firms even after having spent all their capital on imports, still need to buy more (imports), the may have to borrow from other countries, which will lead to debt in the long term. This will be a terrible situation for the firms because, they have to pay debts, and receive capital to pay for imports. If a long time is taken for the debt to be re-payed, the foreign countries may stop lending to those firms, because the foreign countries will have lost faith, in those firms.

Now that the disadvantages are down, let's start with the advantages. Fall in currency. Since the country is exporting fewer goods, the global demand for that country's currency remains low, which results in the currency depreciating (falling). A depreciation means that the currency is cheaper to buy. A cheaper currency means that, foreign firms have to pay less to buy exports from that country, and could possibly lead to an increase in exports from the country. This could fix/reduce the balance of payments deficit.

More Foreign Direct Investment (FDI). FDI is when a foreign firm or individual invests in a country. When a country buy imports, their currency is transferred to the foreign firms. This means that, if they have imported high amounts, means that foreign countries have abundant amount of that country's currency. This makes it easier for foreign firms to invest in that particular country, since the foreign firms already have that country's currency. Higher FDI could drive greater economic growth, because, the country has more capital to invest in developing the economy.

More goods within the economy. In the short term, the country can enjoy a greater quantity of goods for the consumers, and the economy as a whole, because more goods leads to economic growth. Although economic growth is possible, it is still likely that the growth is trivial, largely due to the fact that local goods aren't getting enough demand.

Overall, we can see that although having a balance of payments deficit isn't completely unpleasant for a country, not having one is always better. Also, the disadvantages are more likely to happen than the advantages. This is because, foreign countries won't immediately start buying the country's exports, just because they are cheaper and FDI might not be significantly as well. Meanwhile, high importing is bound to reduce demand for foreign goods, and importing more will definitely reduce capital stock of a country. So overall, a country should import, but should also develop their own goods simultaneously.

ePrabhavnomics blog 43
Originally Published on: 30 June 2019

Heat waves in Europe causes and effects

Summer has just started in Europe, and as it happens in summer it is very warm, however this summer is different compared to other summers. This is because, the temperatures have risen very much, leading to heat waves in Europe. A heatwave is defined as, 'an unseasonably hot period, usually five degrees or more above the average daily maximum, and lasts for a minimum of 3 days.' An example of heatwave in Europe is France, where the temperature has reached to 45.9C, for the first time. Even countries like, Italy, Germany, Spain, Portugal are facing average temperatures over 35C. So what is causing this steep rise in temperatures? Let's find out.

Clear skies. The amount of cloud cover (the fraction of the sky which clouds cover, at a particular location), affects the heat at a particular location. This is because, clouds are able to absorb the heat coming from the sun. Europe during the summer period faces lack of cloud cover, or clear skies, which leads to temperatures increasing to high levels.

Warm air coming from North Africa. Usually Africa's air is warmer than Europe, and hot air usually moves faster than cold air. This is because, higher temperature increases energy of the air particles, causing them to move faster. As mentioned in the introduction, UK hasn't been hit by the heatwave, and this is because it is further away from the source of the warm air. Meanwhile the countries struck by heatwave, are relatively close to North Africa.

Climate change. The average global temperatures are said to be rising every year (called climate change), due to both human and natural causes. This is a possible cause for the heat waves. In fact, the last 4 years, 2015-2018 have been the 4 warmest years. The temperature rise for 2018 is 0.98C, and it is estimated that if this trend continues by 2100, the average temperature rise will be between 3-5C.

So now let's go onto the effects. The population will be affected. Sensitive people, children and elderly are most likely to be affected by high temperatures. This is because, their bodies are unable to bear such heat. In 2003, around 70,000 people died in Europe due to heatwaves. Excess heat can also lead to sleep deprivation and dehydration.

Crops are ruined. Warm weather may be the correct time to grow crops, however excess heat will hinder the crops from growing, specially if the period of the heatwave is long. Apart from crops, even livestock will suffer from this heat. Since in European countries, agriculture comprises only a trivial percentage of economic output, the economy won't face a significant decline in output, but still less crops will mean lower quantity of food for citizens.

Worsening infrastructure. Heatwaves can lead to the melting of roads, (Germany faced this problem recently) which strains the government to built better infrastructure. Railway tracks can bend (buckle) during heatwaves, in fact, in UK during this period, the rail network has lowered the speed limit in order to prevent this problem of rails buckling.

Although Europe having MEDCs (more economically developed countries), it won't face severe problem as LEDCs (less economically developed countries) do (due to heatwaves), such as drought, food shortages, mass migration and (possibly) conflict. This doesn't mean that Europe isn't under threat of anything. This problem of excess heat has just started escalating in Europe, and could lead to unfavourable events if not taken care of. Let's hope this problem is taken care of as soon as possible.

What do you guys think should be done to stop this problem? Let me know in the comments sections, and thanks for reading. Hope you enjoyed!

ePrabhavnomics blog 44
Originally Published on: 7 July 2019

Effects of globalisation on the economy

Globalisation is defined as, 'businesses/organisations developing international influence and starting to operate on international scale.' This means that, many companies have started to operate in many different countries around the world, for example, Starbucks or McDonalds. Both of these companies started off as one single shop, but over the years have expanded to many places around the globe. This is known as globalisation. Globalisation is seen as something positive, because it unites many countries, and usually leads to economic growth (explained in the blog), but it also has disadvantages. This blog will be looking at the pros and cons of globalisation. Hope you enjoy!

Brings major economies together. If a country wants to import goods from another one, the two countries can possibly form a trade agreement (when 2 or more countries agree on terms that helps them trade with each other). Also, when a company wants to set their office in another country, example the ones in the intro, they need to seek approval of that other country. This can lead to a better relationship between the two because, it shows trust between the two.

Free trade is encouraged (read blog 41 to know more about free trade). Free trade is defined as, 'international trade left to its natural course without restrictions.' When globalisation occurs, relationships between countries improves, therefore leading to a greater chance that a country won't impose any restrictions on frequent traders. This helps the economy grow, countries are able to purchase goods, which they aren't able to produce, and that too at competitive prices. If foreign countries have high demand for a local product, firms will employ more workers in order to increase production of that product. This raises both employment, and quantity of goods produced. Although free trade does have some drawbacks (read blog 41), its benefits outweigh its drawbacks (which is excess use of free trade), and overall can benefit the economy.

Can lift LEDCs (less economically developed countries) out of poverty. Free trade aids LEDCs to receive foreign direct investment (FDI), and purchase capital, technology with more ease, which the LEDC can then use to develop the country's infrastructure.

People can gain more knowledge about other countries and their cultures. As globalisation allows countries to come together, it can allow the citizens to learn more about foreign countries. Due to this people will gain more knowledge about the world overall, and probably will find it easier to move around in foreign countries. Also, it is possible that locals may know about a foreign country, and therefore will treat tourists with more tolerance, by taking into account their different culture.

Now that we are done with the pros, let's start with the cons. Environmental damage. Pollution is caused because, air traffic increases, both due to increase in free trade, and possibly more people using airplanes. When the economy grows, people usually get higher incomes, and this increases their possibility of going abroad more often, leading to greater air travel. Also, the extra income can be used to buy cars, which is another major source of pollution. Water pollution is possible, if ship travel is increased. The creation of new firms may lead to deforestation, to create space for the new firms.

Overconsumption. Many goods can be over-consumed by the public, which could lead to a shortage in the future. Similarly, (linking to my previous point), if air travel or cars are over-consumed (meaning lots of people use them, excessively), there will be a significant increase in pollution.

In conclusion, globalisation is something positive for the world, with there being more pros than cons. However, when globalisation occurs, the population should consume only in limit, and be aware of protecting the environment.

Thanks for reading! Hope you enjoyed!

ePrabhavnomics blog 45
Originally Published on: 14 July 2019

Advantages and Disadvantages of having a multinational company (MNC)

As mentioned in the previous blog, globalisation leads to firms expanding their market across the globe, which results in one company being present in several countries. This is usually considered as advantageous because, everyone in the world is able to purchase the same good. However, this can also be a disadvantage both for the company itself and for the citizens. This blog will be exploring how an MNC can have both positives and negatives for the company and citizens. Hope you enjoy!

Starting with the advantages, the first one is, better marketing. Since an MNC has a greater source of revenue, as the company is more widespread around the globe, they have more money to spend on advertising their company. Better/more advertising is more likely to lead to more customers visiting the firm, leading to an increase in the firm's revenue.

Purchasing power of these firms increase. Since the firm's revenue is higher, the firms are able to buy ore capital, like machinery. They are also able to afford the latest technology, which can help them increase their scale of production. Firms can also use this revenue to buy greater quantity of raw material, which can also be used to increase quantity of production in the firm.

An MNC isn't necessarily a monopoly (to know more about a monopoly, read blog 35), since other MNCs can be selling the same good as well, example McDonalds and Burger King, both sell hamburgers. This can be an advantage for consumers as they won't face high prices, this is because, the firms will lose customers if they raise the prices of, as consumers can easily shift to buying from another firm. Also, the company will make sure they sell high quality goods, for the same reason of losing customers.

Rise in employment, across the globe. If the firm, opens new chains (establishments of that market around the globe) in different countries, the market in the foreign country will need workers, therefore employment will rise. Not only that, even if an already existing chain decides to increase production, (possibly due to increased demand), they may employ more workers to increase their production. Increased production also gives the advantage of leading to economic growth.

Moving onto the disadvantages, first one is, difficulty to maintain co-ordination and control. If a decision is made in one of the chains, the decision will have to be communicated to every chain, and due to the firm having possibly many chains around the globe, will find it hard to transfer this decision around.

MNCs could become monopolistic. Although stated in the advantages that, MNCs aren't necessarily monopolies, it is still possible they are, or they might become monopolies. An MNC already has a significant percentage of the market's control (due to its size), and it can easily further increase the market control (by doing the steps mentioned in the advantages), and completely out-power the other firms. If the MNC is able to accomplish this, they can behave like monopolies and implement consumer exploitation, by raising prices and lowering quality.

In MNCs keeping personal contact with customers is harder. Since the number of customers in an MNC are greater than those in a small firm, the employees of an MNC will find greater difficulty in keeping personal contact with customers. This is a drawback for the customers since the employees may not recognise their needs (if they have the same ones). This isn't really a major disadvantages, however the customers won't get any advantages by visiting the store regularly.

In conclusion, there are more advantages than disadvantages of a MNC. Although the number of advantages are higher than the number of disadvantages, the disadvantages could impact the MNC. Therefore, in order for the firm to not face the disadvantages they should; form a good communication system, which can help communication take place quickly, and they should try not to use consumer exploitation.

Thanks for reading! Hope you enjoyed!

ePrabhavnomics blog 46
Originally Published on: 21 July 2019

How do firms grow in size?

As mentioned in the previous two blogs, over time firms expand in size, and serve citizens of several different countries around the globe. We also saw in one of the blogs (blog 45), that the growing of firms mostly gives benefits to the global economy. But, how does this advancement take place in the first place? This blog will be answering these questions. So, hope you enjoy!

Before starting, let's look at the factors which decide how large a firm is; size of capital, volume of sales (how much a firm sells in a period of time), number of employees, level of technology and usage of raw materials. For all these factors, the larger the quantity of each of these factors, the larger the company.

First method of growth is, internal growth. This occurs when a firm increases its size by increasing production, under its current management and control framework. Internal growth can be a result of; investing more in capital and technology, both of which help raise output, or the introduction of a new product in the company, or also when new markets are found overseas to export to.

The next is; external growth. Occurs when two firms join hands (integrate – many forms of integration) to form a single large company. Integration can occur in two ways, one way is when, the firms decide to work together and form a new company. And the second way is, take-over, here one of the companies (let's call it company A, just to avoid confusion) buys at least 50% of another company's ownership shares (company B), this leads to company B losing its identity, and becoming a part of company A.

As mentioned before, the are many types of integration, one of them is; horizontal integration. This is when, two business producing the same goods, and at the same stage of production (different stages of a company, in which they register different growth rates) merge. For example, two car manufacturers merge to become one company.

Next is; vertical integration. This is when, two firms which sell the same product, and are at different stages of production, integrate. An example of vertical integration is, when a car manufacturer joins with a firm making car components. Vertical integration can take place in two directions, one is 'forward integration', which is when a firm takes-over a firm at a higher stage of production. And the other is, 'backward integration', which is when a firm takes-over a firm at a lower-stage of production.

Next is; lateral integration. This is when, two firms, at the same stage of production, and selling different products join hands. This is can be advantageous when compared to the other 3 types of integration, because, here the company can produce a wide range of products. This can be a benefit to the company, since they can get higher revenue, as they are selling several goods. And, if the demand for one of the goods fall, they can still receive revenue from other goods.

Lastly we have; joint venture. In this businesses integrate to share the expense of a project, because it might be too expensive for a single business to bear. One advantage of 'joint venture' is that, businesses don't lose their identity post-integrating.

Overall we can see that there are several ways for a firm to grow. As seen in the blog, most of the ways to grow involves, one firm joining hands with other firms to become one large firm. However a firm can still grow in size by, increasing their production. It all depends on what the firm wants to do.

ePrabhavnomics blog 47
Originally Published on: 28 July 2019

Italy's falling population and its impacts

Population change and population structure (share of a country's population in each age group) is important in deciding, how the economy will change in the future. For example, if a country has a growing population, with most of the people in the young age group, there is a greater chance of higher productivity in the future. Meanwhile, the opposite is true if the country's population is falling. This blog will be exploring how a particular country, Italy, is facing population decline, and examine its impacts. Hope you enjoy!

Last year Italy has registered the lowest birth rate, of 8.5/1000 (which means every 1000 people in the country give an average of 8.5 births), since 1861 and is 4% lower than the birth rate in 2017. Italy also witnessed less than 440,000 births in 2018. The country has been experiencing this decline in birth rate for a long time, however in the recent years (post 2015) the gap between the births and deaths has been very large (with more deaths). This trend, has resulted in a 2% decline in Italy's working population (population aged 15-64) since 2014. Many economists agree that, the country's shrinking population hugely affects its output/GDP (negatively), and its economic growth is expected to remain stagnant.

Apart from just declining birth rate, Italy is also facing lots of 'emigration', which means 'people leaving the country'. In 2018, 157,000 people left the country, which was the highest since 1990. The number of people leaving the country is increasing as the years go by, for example in 2010, only around 80,000 people left Italy. Apart from that, most of the emigrants are in the early stages of their careers, which has led to a 4.3% decrease (from 30.6% to 26.3%) in the number of people between the ages of 25 and 44 in the country, over the last 15 years.

Italy is also experiencing the fastest growing elderly population among all EU countries. For example, in the 1970s Italy's elderly population was around 11%, which was lower than most of the EU countries, while now, Italy's elderly population is 21.7%, when compared to a youthful population of 13.6%. Apart from that, it is predicted that, in 2030 around 27% of Italy's population will be over 64. In terms of elderly population, Italy is second in the world (after Japan). This creates challenges to Italy because, the country's public finances see a drop, due to lower government revenue, as the government has to spend more in pension. In fact Italy spends most of its GDP on pension, across the EU (16.5%). The economy will slow down, because of less workers in the future. The fewer workers will also have the responsibility to look after more elderly people. In 2015 one worker had to look after 34 elderly (on average), in 2070 it is expected to rise to 70 per worker.

Overall, the 3 major problems, which are causing Italy's economy to slow down are; low birth rate, emigration and ageing population. Most, countries that face high ageing population, and low birth rate are MEDCs (more economically developed countries). Emigration however, can be faced by countries of any level of economic development. Also, Italy has to try and solve this problem, otherwise the country will find difficulties in improving, and the future will not be positive for the country's citizens. Few suggestions I have to tackle this issue include; incentivise child birth (like give a bonus for having a child), incentivise the immigration of skilled labour, give job security to women at child bearing age, make child care more affordable.

Thanks for reading! Hope you liked it!

ePrabhavnomics blog 48

Originally Published on: 4 August 2019

Reasons for imposing trade tariffs or quotas

As mentioned in few of my blogs, trade is important for countries, especially because it allows countries to afford goods which they aren't able to produce themselves. However, sometimes a particular country can restrict trade in 3 different ways, for different reasons. This blog will be looking at what these trade restrictions are, and why they are imposed. Hope you like the blog!

The first one is, 'tariffs'. Tariffs can be defined as, 'taxes imposed by the government on imported goods and services', when tariffs are imposed, the foreign firm has to pay extra for importing it's good into the other country, which leads to an increase in the price of the foreign good.

One reason for this restriction can be, 'protecting/boosting domestic firms', if less local goods are bought, the economic growth will decrease (because of less aggregate demand – blog 23 for more info). Therefore the government might place taxes on foreign imports, in order to make them more dearer, leading to an increase in demand for local goods.

Another reason for imposing tariffs is, 'increase the balance of trade', balance of trade calculated by, 'exports – imports', this means that it is better for a country to be exporting more than importing. A tariff raises the price of foreign goods and services, causing imports to fall, exports may not increase, but if imports fall, the difference between exports and imports rises.

'Increasing revenue' the government can impose tariffs for the sole reason of increasing their revenue. As tariffs increase price of goods, the government might impose tariffs on foreign imports only to raise their own revenue.

The next type of restriction is 'non-tariff barriers'. Here the good will have to face some different types of measures (other than tariffs), such as quality check, before entering the local market. The government can restrict can good from being imported if it doesn't meet a particular standard/criteria.

One reason for this restriction includes, 'protecting the population', if a good is of mediocre quality, and is imported without any check, it could negatively affect the local population. For example, stale food, could give illnesses to the population.

Another reason for non-tariff barriers is, 'environmental issues', if a particular good doesn't adhere to environmental standards, the government can stop it from entering their country, in fear of environmental problems.

Last is, 'quotas'. A quota is a restriction to either the quantity or monetary value of a specific good or service that can be imported over a certain period of time, usually over a year. One reason for imposing a quota could be, 'avoiding foreign products from flooding the local market'. If excess of a good is imported to a country, it is possible that, that particular good could gain a significant percentage of the total (local) market share, leaving domestic producers out of business.

Another reasons for quota is, 'boosting/protecting local markets', like tariffs even quotas can be used to avoid international goods from taking over national goods.

Overall, we can see that the major reason for imposing trade restrictions is; to stop foreign firms from taking over local ones. There are other reasons for imposing trade restrictions, such as, increasing trade balance or protecting citizens, however boosting local markets is the main aim, when these trade restrictions are imposed. Any restriction can lead to a disadvantage for the local economy, if the foreign good has a high demand and necessity in the domestic market, however, it can be useful when the foreign good isn't in high demand.

Thanks for reading! Hope you like the blog!

ePrabhavnomics blog 49
Originally Published on: 11 August 2019

Article 370 and 35A and its consequences on Kashmir

The Kashmir issues has been going on for a very long period of time, since 1947, where India, Pakistan and China have been fighting over Kashmir's possession. Recently, this conflict has taken a turn-up in favour of India. This has involved the Prime Minister of India scrapping two major articles, which involve Kashmir, and those article are; Article 370 and Article 35a. This blog will be talking about the significance of the two articles and how their abolition will help India in winning this conflict. Hope you enjoy!

Let's start with explaining the meaning of the two articles. Article 370 allowed Jammu and Kashmir (J&K) to have a separate constitution (constitution – basic principles and laws), a state flag and rights for the state to self-govern. Article 35A granted J&K state's legislature (legislature – group of people in a country who make and change laws) to give its 'permanent residents' unique privileges. A 'permanent resident' is a person who has lived in the state for 10 years and has legally bought immovable property (in the state). Those who aren't 'permanent residents' can't; own a property in J&K, obtain a government job (in J&K) and get any aid from government funds.

Due to the revoking of these two articles, J&K will lose its rights of having a separate constitution. Now J&K will have to adhere to the Constitution of India, just like the rest of the country. So any central law, on any issue in now also applicable to J&K. Also, the people from outside J&K (non-permanent residents) are able to buy property in the state, and reside within the state. Kashmiris will only be allowed to have a single citizenship, previously when the state had it separate laws, the citizens could have a dual citizenship (Indian citizenship and Kashmiri citizenship). Kashmir will no longer be allowed to have a separate flag. Also, J&K's industry will grow, because, as non-residents can purchase property in the state, investment in the state will rise, which will help boost J&K's economy.

Apart from just abolishing J&K's special powers, the government also introduced a Bill (called Jammu and Kashmir Reorganisation Bill, 2019) to divide the state into 2 union territories, which are Jammu and Kashmir, Ladakh. The Bill was successfully passed in the LoK Sabha (lower house of India's parliament) and Rajya Sabha (upper house of India's parliament), with a clear majority. The President has also given approval, after which, J&K is no longer be a state. J&K now legislature, where law and order are decided by the Centre. Ladakh on the other hand has no legislature.

Since this bill has lead to J&K having to follow India's rules and regulations, there is no chance of Pakistan or China trying to claim the state. We are currently unsure about what can happen in the future, since we cannot expect a sudden end to the conflict, in fact there are chances of the conflict getting more heated, because Pakistan and China are unwilling to give up Kashmir.

Overall, despite the bill giving India more power over Kashmir, there are still possibilities of China and Pakistan trying to revolt this decision taken by the government. I believe we have to wait and see what will happen as time goes by. On the whole however, I believe this is a brave and much-needed step taken by India in order to claim Kashmir.

What do you guys think about this step? Let me know.

ePrabhavnomics blog 50
Originally Published on: 18 August 2019

50 Completion – History of my blogs!

Hello everyone! Today I am completing 50 blogs, therefore I have decided that, rather than explaining a new topic or talking about a real life event, I have decided to just talk about few of my past blogs. The selection of blogs is mostly random, and the ones which I have listed below aren't due to any sort of significance. While I write about my previous blogs, I encourage anyone interested to read them on my profile. And, hope you like this blog!

I started by writing about the impacts of 1 rupee equalling 1 US dollar. In the blog I explained that with a stronger currency, India will have benefits such as cheaper imports. Cheaper imports will enable India to have greater access to goods and services which it can't produce (easily) in the country. However, we saw that there are also negative effects to this, and they are; dearer exports, higher labour costs and foreigners will find it harder to invest in

India. Since India is not yet a developed country, this situation of 1 rupee being equal to 1 dollar is not ideal for India.

Later I explained what were the causes and effects of a high youthful population and a high elderly population (blog 6 and 7). In these blogs we saw that, mostly LEDCs (less economically developed countries) face high youthful population, and MEDCs (more economically developed countries) face high elderly population. Lack of knowledge about contraception and family planning was a major cause for high young population, along many others. Meanwhile, in MEDCs good health care lead to high life expectancy, leading to a large elderly population.

Then I went on to talk about the UN (blog 13) and sustainable development in the following blogs. We looked at how the UN formed 17 sustainable goals in order to make the world a better place, and how some have worked out (not completely) and made the world a somewhat better place. Examples of these goals include; No Poverty, Reduced Inequalities, Life Below Water/On Land. In few of my future blogs I also suggested few ways to achieve some of the goals.

In many of my recent blogs I have been talking about trades between countries, and globalisation. In those blogs it can be seen why trading is necessary in order for countries to have access to the goods which they can't produce themselves. I also said that globalisation is beneficial for the world, since it helps unite major economies. However, globalisation can also cause environmental damage.

And my previous (blog 49) spoke about the recent Article 370 and 35A abolished by India in order to gain control over Kashmir. It spoke about how this article will make Kashmir lose its special status of having its own constitution, and Kashmir will be forced to stick to India's rules and regulations. Also region was divided into two union territories; Jammu & Kashmir (J&K) and Ladakh.

Overall, these were few of my previous blogs summarised. As mentioned in the introduction, if any of you is interested in reading them in more detail, I encourage you to go and check them out. Anyways, hope you liked this blog!

ePrabhavnomics blog 51
Originally Published on: 25 August 2019

What if India was never colonised?

India just celebrated its Independence Day 10 days ago (15 August). 15 August marked the end of British rule on India, who ruled India for more than 200 years. It was definitely a wonderful day for Indians. However, what would have happened if the British never ruled India in the first place. How would India have been different compared to what it is today? In this blog I will be explaining what would be India's situation today if the British never ruled it. Hope you like it. PS: This blog doesn't intend to condemn any nation.

The country would have been richer. According to a book, 'Poverty and Un-British Rule in India', written by Dadabhai Navroji, the wealth drained by the British from India amounted to 4 million pounds every year (200 years ago ..which would have resulted in billions today). So it is fair to say that India would have had much more wealth if it was never ruled by the British. An example of a something precious which was taken from India by the British was, the Kohinoor Diamond. It is on public display in the Jewel House, located in the Tower of London, and is seen by million of people every year. Since 1947 (India's Independence) many governments such as; India, Pakistan, Iran and Afghanistan have claimed ownership of the Kohinoor and requested UK to return it, however UK's government claims to have legally obtained it (in the Last Treaty of Lahore) and never returned it to India.

Indian industries would have been grown better. Most of Britain's industrial revolution is due to India's deindustrialization, for example India's textile industry was nearly destroyed, and Indian material was used to produce textiles in Britain. Which Britain then sold back to the whole world (including India). Also the British imposed high taxes on industrial workers in the country, which caused poverty to rise in the country. In conclusion we can say that, India could have been the world's largest textile exporter.

Unification of the nation. One of the major reason for the British being able to capture India was the fact that it was not unified, and it is possible that India could have still had 100s of princely states if not for the British rule. When India was under Britain's rule, many freedom fighters fought for the whole nation's freedom, which is a possible reason why India became unified post-independence.

Democracy in the country. India wasn't such a democratic country pre British rule, and it is the British who introduced Parliamentary election in the country, with the 'Indian Councils Act 1861'. This was the first time Indians could vote for the Lok

Sabha (Indian Parliament). India may have remained a monarchy without the electoral systems which the British introduced to the country.

Overall we can say that, the British rule did negatively affect the country, however there were some positive things which the British helped our country achieve (like the electoral systems). One also cannot deny that quite a lot of India's technological advancements like; railways, airways, setting up telegraph posts is due to the British, and also India has developed in few fields due to the British. However, it is not said that without the British rule India wouldn't have been able to progress in those fields, in fact I believe without the British rule we could have advanced in those areas better/more. Especially because, without the rule our country's citizens wouldn't have had to face brutal conditions. Also, India would have been wealthier, therefore it would have had more resources to develop.

That's all, hope you liked this blog. What is your opinion on this topic?

ePrabhavnomics blog 52
Originally Published on: 1 September 2019

Festivals and their impact on the economy

Festival season is right around the corner in India, with many festivals taking place in the next few months, like Ganesh Chaturthi, Navrathri, and Diwali. This will be the same in the western world, with Halloween, Thanksgiving and Christmas coming up in the next few months. The festival season will definitely be having some sort of impact on the economy, which is what we will be analysing in this blog. So, hope you like this blog!

Usually, during the festive season people get holidays, and possibly even get bonuses from office. Therefore people have more time, and more spending power, which makes it more likely for them to increase spending. Since aggregate demand (total demand for a countries' goods and services) rises, due to greater spending from citizens, manufactures are able to increase revenue, and also will be able to increase output in the future, due to this increased revenue. Increased output leads to economic growth of the country.

Some markets can see a boost during this period, when during the rest of the year they don't get much products sold. An example of an market where this could occur is; stores that sell decorations, many sweet & gift shops. Although there can be high demand for these markets during the other periods of the year, they usually see a significant rise during the festive seasons, especially because, these products mentioned above are mostly used during festivals. This is a positive for the producers of these goods.

Certain festivals can allow a country's culture to be more familiar around the world, which can lead to increased tourism to that country, since people can be curious to know more about the culture. Increased tourism to a country helps that country's economy to grow, again due to increased aggregate demand.

Exports might increase, since people of a particular nationality might be living abroad. It is possible that, the decorations or material required for a particular festival may not be available abroad, thus individual residing in foreign nations may require the nation of origin (the country where the festival originates) to export the necessary festival material to their nation of residence. When exports take place, money is sent to the exporting country, which will help the exporting country's economy to grow (again due to increase in aggregate demand).

Festivals don't necessarily only have a positive impact on the public, it is possible that festivals can cause environmental damage. For example, in India every year post Diwali, many major cities face heavy air pollution due to bursting of fire crackers. This affects both the population, and it puts strain on the government, because, they have to spend lots of money to improve the countries' health care, the government will therefore have to neglect other aspects of the economy for health care, which therefore could lead to the economy slightly slowing down. Not every festival leads to environmental damage, like mentioned above, however if many people attend the festival there can still be problems like; littering in the streets and traffic (leading to air pollution).

Overall, we can see that festivals usually lead to positive effects, and can help boost the economy, and can lead to a rise in tourism in the country. However, there can still be many environmental problems caused during festivals, especially if lots of people attend the festival. However I also believe that, the extra revenue generated in the economy during festive period can possibly be used to look after the environmental problems, and implement any solutions.

Anyways hope you liked the blog! Wishing a happy Ganesh Chaturthi to every Indian reading this!

<u>ePrabhavnomics blog 53</u>
Originally Published on: 8 September 2019

Impacts of a Space Program on a country's economy

Just recently, India has carried out its second lunar exploration mission (Chandrayaan-2), which was also the first mission which explored the Lunar South Pole. This was also the Indian Space Research Organisation (ISRO)'s 3rd extraterrestrial exploration mission, after the Chandrayaan-1 (first lunar exploration mission) in 2008, and the Mars Orbiter Mission (or Mangalayaan) in 2013/14. The Chandrayaan-2 wasn't completely successful, since the scientists lost communication with the space craft (the Vikram lander) 2.1km before landing. However, it is not to be forgotten that the Vikram lander successfully travelled 3.844 lakh km (384.4 thousand km). And let's hope that the next lunar exploration mission carried out by ISRO becomes a success. Anyways, onto this blog, today's blog will be talking about how a Space Program can impact a country's economy. So, hope you like it!

Starting with the positives, space exploration can help reduce problems faced on Earth. This means that, some resources can be found on other planets, which can be brought back to Earth. For example, iron, nickel, tungsten, cobalt and many more are found on some other planet. This helps a country's economy since the country could solve its problems of lack of resources with space exploration. A country without a space program might have to consult with other countries to the resources they found from space. However, the origin country might benefit if foreign countries buy the resources they found from space, because, when they export the resources they get money in return.

Space exploration helps us prepare for potential threats. Examples of dangers from our solar system include; asteroids and comets, both of them can easily destroy our planet with a single collision. With space exploration we can easily spot a hazard like this much way before it takes place and work on avoiding it. Space exploration can also help us track down when solar/lunar eclipses are going to happen, both of which can harm human sight.

Apart saving us from hazards in our solar system, space exploration also helps us predict the weather, with the use of satellites, if a country doesn't have a satellite, they can ask a country which does (have a satellite) to share any space related information. This is a gain for the country with the satellite, because they are using their service to help another country. When a particular country's good or service is used (by any country), that particular country's economy grows.

When a mission is planned, one has to invest in that project, and the amount invested in the project will be later used in buying raw material to build the satellite/rocket and any technical aspect required. This investment means that the country's goods are being used, which as mentioned in the previous paragraph is a boon for a country's economy to grow.

Now, let's see some negative points of Space Programs. Space exploration has high costs. Most of the space exploration organisations are public, (government owned), which means that the government finances the projects. They are also very expensive to carry out, and probably the government may not have enough revenue to finance these projects, and might feel that it is better to invest in some other area in the economy than for the space exploration. It is possible for the scientists to carry out the space programs with a lower budget, however it will be harder to gain success with this. Also, if the mission is unsuccessful the government will face a huge loss, which is also a loss for the economy as a whole.

Overall, space programs have a positive impact on the economy, and also on the globe as a whole. However, it their high costs can be a huge drawback, especially if they are unable to afford that much budget. But despite this problem, if the scientists are able to find a way to carry out the mission, with a lower cost, the huge budget of the mission will not affect the progress of the mission. But it is not to be forgotten that carrying out any space mission is a huge task, and even one mistake could lead to a failure of the mission. Anyways, hope you liked this blog! Thanks for reading!

ePrabhavnomics blog 54

Originally Published on: 15 September 2019

The total value of the World Economy, and its breakdown.

Every country's economy's size depends on the total number of goods and services they produce over the period of one year. The monetary value of all goods and services is shown by the GDP (gross domestic product) of the country. And obviously, the countries with higher GDP are considered the ones with a bigger economy (not necessarily richer). If the total GDP is divided by the total population of the country, the average wealth of every individual in the country can be seen, and it is called GDP per capita. This blog will only be looking at total GDP of the country, and looking at major economies and their contribution to the total global GDP.

Starting off, the value of the world's total economy is $86 trillion. Out of this, the top 15 economies contribute to around 75% of the world's total GDP, a cumulative total of $64.42 trillion. With a further breakdown, the top 5 economies of the world are; the United States, China, Japan, Germany and the United Kingdom. Their total (total of top 5) contributes to 67.5% of the total world's economy. Below I will show their total GDP values, and their percentage contributions to the world economy. (PS: I haven't add their percentages to calculate their contribution, but their actual GDP values).

1)	**United States**	$20.49 trillion	23.89%
2)	**China**	$13.61 trillion	15.86%
3)	**Japan**	$4.97 trillion	5.79%
4)	**Germany**	$4 trillion	4.66%
5)	**United Kingdom**	$2.83 trillion	3.29%

The other 10 countries in the Top 15 economies are; France, India, Italy, Brazil, Canada, Russia, Korea, Australia, Spain and Mexico.

The continent in the world which has the highest GDP is 'Asia'. Asia has a total GDP of $28.17 trillion and contributes to 32.7% of the global GDP. In second place we have 'Europe', with a total GDP of $19.15 trillion, and contributing to 22.3% of the total GDP. Next is 'Latin America and Caribbean', with a total GDP of $4.24 trillion and contribute to roughly 5% of the total world GDP.

If we break down the contribution to GDP by sorting out countries in terms of 'income levels', we see that 'High income countries' contribute to 63.1% of the total world GDP and a total of $54.1 trillion. Meanwhile the 'low income countries' only have $0.6 trillion dollars worth of GDP and contribute only 0.7% of the total world's GDP. This shows the inequality in the world, and the huge gap between the rich and the poor.

Overall, this is the breakdown of the world's total $86 trillion GDP. We saw in this blog which countries have the highest GDP, which continent has the highest GDP and the countries of which economic level have the highest share of the world's GDP. Let's hope that in the future every country's GDP is significantly higher than now, and the inequality between the high income and low income countries reduces.

Anyways, thanks for reading! Hope you liked it!

ePrabhavnomics blog 55

Originally Published on: 22 September 2019

Major economies in 2030

In last week's blog we saw which are the current major economies in the world, and what portion of the total world GDP ($86 trillion) do these economies account for. Meanwhile in today's blog we will be looking at which countries will be major economies in 2030, and what will be total GDP of the world be in 2030. I will also be comparing it with the present scenario, just so you can see the differences. So hope you enjoy this blog. PS: This figures which I will present in the blog are just predictions and may turn out to be false.

So, the top 5 economies are projected to be; China, India, US, Indonesia and Turkey. These 5 economies together will comprise at total of $160.7 trillion, which is even higher than the total of the whole world today. Although the projected figures of the world economy in 2030 are not available yet, we can imagine how much larger it will be in 2030, especially when compared to what it is today. Below is a table showing the top 5 economies and their current and expected (2030) GDP.

Rank	Country (current rank)	Current GDP	2030 Projected GDP (total % growth)
1	China (2)	$13.61 trillion	$64.2 trillion (372%)
2	India (5)	$2.73 trillion	$46.3 trillion (1596%)
3	United States (1)	$20.49 trillion	$31 trillion (51%)
4	Indonesia (16)	$1.1 trillion	$10 trillion (809%)
5	Turkey (20)	$0.74 trillion	$9.1 trillion (1130%)

As you can see from the table, every economy (except United States) will experience an exponential growth in their economy, two other economies which will see a huge growth include; Egypt and Brazil. Egypt which currently has a total GDP of $0.3 trillion and is on rank 40, will move to rank 7 in 2030 and have a total of $8.2 trillion. This is an increase of over 2000%. Meanwhile Brazil which currently has a total GDP of $1.87 trillion and is on rank 9, will have $8.2 trillion in 2030 (over 300% growth), and will move to rank 6.

Although developed countries like the United States, Germany and Japan will still have growing economies, their growth will be lower than that of developing economies. According to the projection Japan will be ranked 9, compared to rank 3 today and Germany will be ranked 10, compared to rank 4 today. Japan's current GDP is $4.97 trillion, and it is projected to be $7.2 trillion in 2030, this is only a 45% increase. Germany's current GDP is $4 trillion, and it is expected to reach $6.9 trillion in 2030, and this is a 72.5% increase.

Overall, the reasons for such trends is possibly due to the closing gap between the rich and the poor. Also, developing economies are the ones which are in need of development, so there is a higher possibility for economic growth to take place in developing countries. If Developing countries get hold of resources which developed countries already have, their economy will hugely grow, meanwhile developed countries already have most of the resources, and therefore are less likely to grow fast.

Hope you liked this blog! Thanks for reading!

ePrabhavnomics blog 56
Originally Published on: 29 September 2019

US – China Trade War and its impacts

Every country trades goods with other countries, especially giving the goods to the countries which lack them and need them. However, some countries may want other countries to stop trading with them, for several different reasons, therefore they can impose a trade restriction on the other country, examples include; tariff (a tax which the exporting country has to pay before the goods enters the other country) or a quota (when a country limits the physical quantity of goods that can be imported over a year). However, it is possible that, when a country places a tariff or quota on another country, the other country does the same. When this happens, it is called a trade war between the two countries. A trade war currently taking place is the; US – China trade war, and its impacts on both countries and the world.

Both of these countries will face negative consequences due to this trade war. This is mainly because, they are major trade partners. Significant number of US imports are from China, it is the second country which the US buys from (EU as a whole being ranked one). US is the country where China exports mostly to, this trade war definitely is a negative for China, since it will export less, therefore its economy will grow slower. The slowing down of China's economy is because, since less of its exports are bought, China's aggregate demand (AD – total demand for a country's goods and services) will fall. Although US exports less to China (than China to US), the US will also face a slower growing economy, due to this trade war, for the same reason as China.

This trade war can lead to a decline in the global economic growth. This is mainly because, the US and China are two major economies, and they have reduced trading with each other, the global economy is experiencing a decline in overall trade, which in turn is causing an economic slowdown. Globally, also the foreign direct investment has fallen. This trade war has affected many countries like Germany, even though it has good trade relations with both China and the US. Several other countries like; the UK, Germany (and the EU as a whole), Japan and South Korea have seen reductions in manufacturing in 2019. These countries are facing losses due to the trade war because, these countries rely quite heavily on trade for economic development, and since the global trade has dropped, these countries face economic slowdown.

Despite this, there are many emerging countries that can benefit from this trade war. Examples of countries include; Vietnam, that can see a 33% increase in exports to the US. Next is Bangladesh, which can see a 13% increase in exports to US. The countries that can benefit from this trade war are; Malaysia, Thailand and the

Philippines. The reason for these countries benefitting, is that, these countries are low-cost exports, which makes them more attractive for US firms. You can see that most of the emerged economies are the ones facing losses from this trade war, and most emerging economies are benefitting.

Overall, there are more countries are harmed by this trade war, when compared to those profiting from it. In my opinion, the trade war should end, since it is has more disadvantages compared to advantages. I would also like it if the benefitting countries continue to grow fast, and experience lots of exports even after the trade war comes to an end.

Hope you like this blog! What are your views on this trade war? Let me know.

ePrabhavnomics blog 57
Originally Published on: 6 October 2019

How a No-Deal Brexit could affect the world economy

Since 23 June 2016 (when people voted for the UK to leave the European Union (EU)), Brexit has been a much-talked about topic, many people wanting to change their opinion and not wanting the UK to leave the EU, while others talking about the uncertainty of when Brexit is going to take place. Now after 3 deadline extensions, Brexit is scheduled to take place on 31 October 2019 and, there are high chances that a 'No-Deal Brexit' takes place. In this blog we will talking about what a 'No-Deal

Brexit' is, and how it will affect the world economy. Hope you like this blog!

A 'No-Deal Brexit' means that the UK will withdraw from the EU, without any special agreement about EU and UK's relationship, (such as a trade pact between the UK and EU, or an agreement of how their companies can work together) in the future.

One of the negative impacts of a 'no-deal Brexit' is that; the trade between UK and EU can drastically drop. The UK and the EU trade excessively with each other, and if trade between them dips it could affect the global economy. This is because, when trade drops, aggregate demand (AD) for a countries' goods falls. AD is one of the major factors affecting economic growth, because it shows the total earnings of a country during a year, and the more a country earns in a year, the bigger the economy becomes. Bearing in mind the ongoing US-China trade war (more explanation in blog 56), which had already caused trade between US and China to plummet and has affected many countries, a 'no-deal Brexit' could therefore cause the global economic growth to slow down even more. EU countries like Germany especially, (which are already affected by the US-China trade war) will face the most number of repercussions.

The UK will be the most harmed due to a 'no-deal Brexit', since it imports most of its goods from the EU. UK's economy is expected to slowdown by 3% if a 'no-deal Brexit' takes place. The UK may have to face some EU tariffs or go through customs when importing EU goods, which will cause its balance of payments (monetary value of; exports minus imports) to go towards a bigger deficit, and there will be delays (due to customs). Even if UK will find it harder to get EU goods, it won't have to any longer pay its contribution to the EU, this could stop its budget from seeing a huge drop.

It is possible that with a 'no-deal Brexit' the other EU countries may be unwilling to give their jobs to UK workers.

Unemployment will lead to a lower standard of living for these people, which is never good for a country. Similarly, EU workers working in the UK may face unemployment, it is also possible that future EU workers may stop coming to the UK for finding work, which will lead to a labour shortage in the UK.

Post-Brexit the pound's value will fall, this is a disadvantage for the US because they will find it dearer to export their goods to the UK. The US sectors that export the most to the UK will face the biggest loss. UK is on rank 4, when it comes to countries receiving most US exports.

Overall you can see how a 'No-Deal Brexit' will lead to several negative consequences to the global economy and individual countries. Therefore let's hope that a 'No-Deal Brexit' doesn't take place. Since Brexit is unfortunately inevitable now, and it will have consequences (blog 30 and 31 have them in more detail) it would be better if its fallouts are reduced.

What are you views on this topic? Let me know. Hope you liked this blog.

<u>ePrabhavnomics blog 58</u>
Originally Published on: 13 October 2019

UK prime minister's Final Brexit Offer to European Union

As you all know Brexit is going to take place at the end of this month (31 October), and before it takes place many things need to take place, such as deals between the UK and the European Union (EU). In my blog last week (blog 57) I wrote about what would happen if the EU and UK didn't agree on a deal before Brexit (called 'No-Deal Brexit). And you can see if there is a 'No-Deal Brexit' the consequences for the especially the UK and the EU will be dire. The Prime Minister of the UK has recently finalised a Brexit deal to the EU. This blog will be analysing the deal.

The PM's plan involves removing Northern Ireland from EU's custom union (an agreement made by several countries to remove any trade restrictions among them) along with the rest of the UK, and involve checks on goods exported and imported to Northern Ireland. However, Northern Ireland will follow the same rules on goods, as the EU does, until December 2020 (only if Northern Ireland's Parliament agrees), which is the end of the transition period. The transition period is a period post-Brexit during which the UK and EU will still have their past agreements (like trade agreements) in place.

Then (after December 2020), every four years the politicians of Northern Ireland can vote on whether they want to continue to follow the same rules as the EU, or if they want to stop following the rules and then join the rest of the UK.

Since Northern Ireland will continue following the same rules as the EU, there will be new borders post-Brexit. There will be a custom border (an area where goods go for controls) between Northern Ireland and Ireland. The government also proposes to keep an area on the island of Ireland (also known as the; all-island regulatory zone) where custom checks will take place. And there will be a regulatory border (a border where even people will need visa to enter) between Northern Ireland and Great Britain.

The agreement also proposes for custom checks (between Northern Ireland and Great Britain) to take place electronically, and with the quantity of physical checks which need to be conducted at the premises of the traders or other locations within the supply chain. Meanwhile, Northern Ireland and Ireland are part of different custom territories, and have custom control in place, when they trade goods with each other.

These are few key events that will take place before Brexit; 14 October – the government will use the Queen's speech to set out its laws. The speech will later be debated by MPs during the week. 17 October – It will be the beginning of the 2 day summit of the EU leaders (in Brussels). Last scheduled meeting before Brexit deadline. 19 October – Brexit deal will be voted in Parliament. 31 October – Day UK will withdraw from the EU (as of now).

Overall, this is what the PM's final Brexit offer was, to the EU. In my opinion it is a not such a reasonable offer since, the UK will have difficulty in getting goods from any EU country or Northern Ireland. It is to be seen whether the EU will accept this offer or not. The UK PM has said that if the deal is not agreed on 19 October, Brexit's date will be extended again, this contradicts the PM's previous statements were he said he won't extend Brexit's date after 31 October. Anyways, lets see what happens, because it will be interesting to see how the EU reacts to this deal.

Hope you liked this blog! Thanks for reading!

ePrabhavnomics blog 59
Originally Published on: 20 October 2019

Advantages and Disadvantages of trade blocs

When neighbouring countries (usually), trade with each other very regularly, it is possible for them to from trade agreements between each other. These agreements can include; free trade amongst them (no tariffs or quotas), a common external tariff on non-members of the bloc, common rules and regulations among the members and no border checks. Having a trade bloc can have both advantages and disadvantages for members and non-members. This blog will be looking at what the pros and cons of a trade bloc. Hope you like it! PS, examples of existing trade blocs include; the European Union (EU) and North Atlantic Free Trade Association (NAFTA- between US, Canada and Mexico).

Starting with the advantages, the first one we have is; cheaper goods for other members. Without any tariffs, the goods will be much cheaper to buy, and this is an advantage for both the exporting country and the importing country. The importing country will face more ease to buy the goods, and the exporting country will be able to increase its sales (since lower price increases demand) and yield profits.

More trade can lead to specialisation. Specialisation is when a person or country (in this case), concentrates on a particular skill and becomes an expert in that skill. In this case, if a country exports large amounts of a good, it can decide to specialise in that good. Due to specialisation, it can achieve 'economies of scale' (increase output, but keep average production costs low). Economies of scale is possible because, due to specialisation, the workers become more efficient at their task, and therefore are able to produce more.

If 'less economically developed countries' (LEDCs) join trade blocs with 'more economically developed countries' (MEDCs), the LEDCs can benefit from inward investment (when people outside a country, invest in that country). Inward invest can allow the LEDCs to increase their total GDP, causing them to face economic growth. LEDCs can also benefit from higher trade opportunities, which will also lead to economic growth.

Increase competition. Due to no-tariffs every country will focus on improving their goods' quality, and will reduce the price, in order to get higher demand for their goods. Similarly, non-members will also work on producing better quality goods, and cutting their prices, in order to again increase demand for their goods. This will benefit the consumers worldwide, since they can buy cheap high quality goods.

Now onto the disadvantages. Lack of sovereignty. Whenever a trading bloc makes a decision, it has to be followed by every country in the bloc. Some countries may not be happy with this decision, but will be forced to follow it. No country can make a trade decision that is applicable only to that country.

Interdependence. Countries may become too dependent on the free trade received by other countries of that bloc. Therefore, if there is high demand for a country's exports, and that country faces a natural disaster or any other problem, which causes its production of that good to fall, it will lead to other countries in the bloc facing damages as well. This is because, other countries can't buy goods which they may need, and the country facing the disaster will lose on lots of output.

Overall, forming trade blocs creates more advantages than disadvantages, this therefore tells us that free trade is generally beneficial to all countries. However, these cons of blocs can be overcome by, countries not becoming too dependent on trade from other bloc members. Countries should also be ready to give up their sovereignty, and accept what is decided by the trade bloc.

This is all. Hope you liked the blog!

ePrabhavnomics blog 60
Originally Published on: 27 October 2019

Effects of remittances on the economy of destination

Migration is a common act, with several people leaving a country and entering another everyday. Usually, when people from the working population (age 15-64), go to a foreign country to find work (due to more opportunities abroad), and their family stays in the home country, it is possible for the workers to send back money to their home country. The money sent to the home country is known as, 'remittances'. This blog will talk about how remittances can affect the economy of the country of destination (where remittances are sent to). Hope you like it!

Remittances are usually sent from 'more economically developed countries' (MEDCs) to 'less economically developed countries' (LEDCs), and are considered as a form of foreign investment in LEDCs. Families in LEDCs who receive remittances, see an increase in the amount of money they have available to spend. This allows these families to have a higher standard of living, especially since the goods and services are more affordable to them.

Since remittances are a form of investment in the economy, remittances can help the destination country's total GDP to increase, which in turn raises income levels in the country. The rise in GDP will also help the country as a whole to boost its infrastructure, as the government will spend more in the economy. Due to higher income levels, the poverty level and inequality in the country can fall. Even if the family receiving the remittances may not be poor, as they spend their remittances in the economy, their money can later get to poorer people, as it circulates throughout the economy.

Although remittances help increase an LEDC's GDP, it still has some negative effects on the country. For example, they can lead to people being overdependent on them. Due to this over-dependence, workers still inside the country may decide to work less, since they will anyways get remittances which will help contribute to the economy, and their income. Although the size of the remittances can be high, the country's production of goods and services will fall, and in the longer run if remittances fall, the country will have fewer goods and services for the economy.

Many family members may believe that the workers are better off; migrating to an MEDC, earning more and sending his income back, rather than him staying in their national country and earning locally. This leads to a smaller working force in the country, leading to lower production of local goods and services. Like the previous point, although remittances will help the economy grow/remain stable, fewer goods and services in the economy will be detrimental for the economy.

Remittances lead to the a currency appreciation (increase in value), due to greater demand for the currency. When investing in the country, the people from abroad need to buy the local currency, which is why the demand for that currency increases. Anyways, when the currency appreciates, the exports from that country seem dearer to foreign countries, therefore fewer exports are bought. Import prices are cheaper, and therefore more imports are bought. This overall is a negative for the country, since they are spending more money than receiving.

Overall, remittances can prove to a huge advantage to LEDCs, by aiding them to increase GDP, and reduce poverty/inequality levels. However, it also increases an LEDC's dependency on them, and could lead to a dip in labour participation in that LEDC. Therefore, a country should take full benefit of remittances, however shouldn't become too overly dependent on them, and should continue to work towards increasing quantity of goods and services in their own country.

ePrabhavnomics blog 61
Originally Published on: 3 November 2019

Why GDP isn't a good way to measure standard of living?

Gross domestic product (GDP), is defined as, the monetary value of the total number of goods and services produced by a country over the period of one year. Whenever GDP of a country rises, it is said that the country has undergone economic growth. The country's average income (GDP per capita) is calculated by dividing total GDP with total population of the country, therefore a rise in GDP means a rise in average income of that country, and the country has become richer. However, GDP still has some shortcomings which leads to it becoming less reliable when measuring standard of living. This blog will be exploring some of the reasons why GDP is not 100% dependable. Hope you like the blog!

GDP doesn't take into account the cost of living of the country, nor inflation. The final value of GDP per capita is only 'total GDP divided by total population', which tells us what the person on average earns. However, GDP per capita doesn't take into account people's cost of living (cost of living only measures costs of necessities like; housing, food, clothes), therefore it doesn't tell us how much of the income is spent on necessities and how much can be used for luxuries. Inflation isn't considered in GDP, therefore we again don't know the cost faced by the citizens when buying necessities/luxuries.

GDP doesn't consider income equality around the economy. The GDP per capita of the country may be high, but that doesn't necessarily mean everyone is rich. It is possible that, the richest 5-10% people have over 60% of the total GDP, and the rest 90-95% are left with the remaining 40% of GDP (this is a hypothetical example, there may or may not be a country with this income distribution), however the rest of the world is unaware of this, and this country is considered rich by everyone.

Costs of economic growth aren't taken into account in GDP. Economic growth does have some negative effects (blog 32 mentions all of them), and GDP doesn't count them in the final value. Pollution is an example of a negative consequence of economic growth, (because when factories produce more they let out more carbon emissions), and it leads to several health problems, which overall lowers standard of living. It is possible that two countries have the same GDP per capita, but one has pollution problems the other doesn't, so the country with no pollution has better standard of living. Due to the costs not being taken into account, we don't get the true picture of the economic development that has taken place in the country, because if pollution has remained high over the years, even if GDP has risen significantly, the country hasn't necessarily developed economically.

GDP doesn't measure happiness of a country. While it is true that higher GDP per capita does mean higher affordability (if costs of living are the same everywhere), however, it doesn't mean people are happier. It is possible that people work for greater hours to produce higher GDP, and spend fewer hours on vacation. Meanwhile, another country can have a slightly lower GDP, but with much less hours at work. This makes the people of the 2nd country happier, because they spend longer in holidays, and they still produce close to the same as the 1st country.

GDP doesn't show the variety of goods produced. It is possible that a country (Country A) produces excessive amounts of the same good, and minimal outputs of other goods. Meanwhile Country B, produces a similar output of all goods. Even if Country A has a greater GDP than Country B, it can be said that country B is better-off, because the people have greater choice than Country A. However, one can also argue that Country A can specialise itself in the good it produces high quantities of, and the world can buy that good from Country A, which helps Country A see economic growth.

Overall, GDP does tell us the total value of a country's economy and can be used to calculate the economic growth taken place. However, it doesn't really help to measure a country's (income) equality and doesn't tell us the overall standards of living in the country. Hope you liked this blog! Next week's blog will be on alternative indicators to measure standards of living.

ePrabhavnomics blog 62

Originally Published on: 10 November 2019

Alternate indicators to measure standards of living

Last week I wrote a blog on why gross domestic product, (GDP) isn't a good indicator to use when looking at standards of living in a country, and it was majorly because GDP doesn't consider several things in its final value, such as, cost of living, inflation in the country and income equality, to name a few. GDP therefore, alone doesn't give the full picture of a country's economic status. This blog will be looking at few other measures which can be used other than GDP. So, hope you like it! PS: GDP is a good indicator to use when looking at the value of the economy and how much the value grew/declined, however there are better indicators when measuring economic status in the country.

First one is; Income equality. It is important to look at how equal the distribution of income is amongst the population. A country with a high total GDP can still have a very unequal income distribution, and therefore lots of poverty. There is an index called as the 'Gini Index', which gives a value between 0 and 1 to every country according to their levels of inequality. A value of 0 means perfect equality, everyone has the same income, and 1 means maximum inequality, example, India Gini Index is, 0.339. In order to understand the levels of development in a country, the Gini Index has to be compared with GDP (per capita), to check if the (un)equal income is high or low. If a country has a high GDP (per capita) and a low Gini Index it is highly economically developed.

Life Expectancy and infant mortality rate. Life expectancy measures how long a person can expect to live for, based on their year of birth, if death rates at each age remain constant in the future. This tells us the quality of health care in the country. If a country has a higher life expectancy, this means the health care system in the country is very well developed, meanwhile the same vice-versa. Infant mortality rate measures how many children (out of 1000 born every year), will die before turning 1. If a country has a good health care system, the infant mortality rate will be lower, as infants can get better sources of medical support.

The Consumer Price Index (CPI). The CPI measures the weighted average prices of a basket of consumer goods and services. These goods and services can include; food, housing, education and many more. When the price of any good changes, the average is recalculated, and the new CPI is found, a change in CPI means a change in living costs. CPI can also be used to find levels of inflation. CPI and GDP together can help calculated how much spare income people have after covering costs of life. If a country has a high GDP (per capita), and low CPI, that country is highly economically developed. However, it is also to be noted that, as GDP increases, CPI also increases. This is because, when

GDP increases, people usually have higher income, meaning their consumption increases, when consumption increases firms raise prices.

The Human Development Index (HDI). HDI is a composite indicator, that measures the overall level of development in a country, by averaging 3 major things that influence a country's standard of living; health, education and wealth. It measures levels of health of a country by looking at the country's 'Life Expectancy'. The levels of education by looking at 'Mean years of schooling' (MYS) and 'Expected years of schooling' (EYS). Therefore it takes into account adult literacy (MYS), and child literacy (EYS). It looks at a country's wealth by looking at its GDP per capita. Although HDI doesn't consider GDP's weaknesses, HDI can be considered reliable because, since these 3 factors are positively correlated, if one of them is high, it is highly likely the other two are also high. HDI gives every country a value from 0 to 1, which 1 being most developed, example, Italy HDI is 0.880. Higher HDI value, the better the country. Overall, HDI can accurately give us an accurate picture of a country's development status.

Overall, these were few of the indicators which I believe can measure standards of living of a country better than GDP. Before concluding I would like to mention some indicators missing from this list that deserve a mention, they are; environmental quality (air pollution for example can reduce quality of life), access to drinking water (higher in more developed countries), efficiency of transportation (if people live in congested areas, they will find it harder to move around, and this could reduce quality of life).

Anyways, thanks for reading. Hope you liked this blog!

ePrabhavnomics blog 63
Originally Published on: 17 November 2019

Economics impacts of walking

Walking is an important everyday activity. You might have to walk to get around, or you might do it as an exercise. Whatever it is, you may be shocked to hear that walking can help the world economy to grow. Confused? Well, this blog will be explaining how some extra walking can actually lead to a faster economic growth. So, hope you enjoy reading this blog!

Walking usually help you become healthier. Some health benefits of walking include: weight loss, reduces risk of diabetes, improves heart health, and many more. And, every year 5 million people die due to physical inactivity. This is not necessarily true 100% of the times, however most of the times, increasing the number of steps walked everyday helps improve your health. Better health of workers makes them more likely to increase their productivity (rate at which goods are made). Increased productivity leads greater output (number of goods produced), since goods are made at a faster rate. Greater output leads to economic growth.

Healthier people also means less sickness, and which means less absences from work. Lesser absences means that all the workers are present at work most of the time. More workers leads to greater output being produced on a daily basis.

A healthier lifestyle usually means lower risk of death. If people die at an older age, they can continue working for longer. This means that the number of people in the workforce remains high, and this increases the possibility of increasing output. Remember, even if the workers are quite old, if they are healthy (from the walking), they might still be able to produce at the same rate, if not a much lower one.

Even if walking, and a healthier life doesn't lead to higher productivity, and economic growth, a healthier life raises quality of living. Having a higher quality of living is important for everyone because, it makes you happier, and you have to worry less about your health. Although a better quality of living doesn't lead to an economic growth, it allows the country as a whole to develop.

Walking more also helps to protect the environment. If everyone decides to use their car less, and to increase walking, it could help to significantly reduce the amount of air pollution in the country. Air pollution leads to several health issues, such as, respiratory disease, skin damage, headache, to name a few. Therefore, a reduction in air pollution means a better lifestyle overall for the population. More walking also leads to a lower density of traffic on the street. Less traffic jams can lead to lower stress and anxiety in the people.

Overall, you can see that walking helps improve a person's health in several ways. This improved health of a person is a boon in helping to improve the country's quality of life or lead to an economic growth. Therefore my advice to all of you is, 'walk more and help the economy grow'.

If you are wondering how much benefit walking does to the economy, I will tell you that, by 2050, if the least active people decide to walk for at least 150 minutes a week, the world GDP can increase from between US$314 billion to US$446 billion.

Hope you liked this blog! Thanks for reading! Happy walking to everyone!

ePrabhavnomics blog 64
Originally Published on: 24 November 2019

Italy's new tax on plastic & sugar drinks and its effects

Taxes aren't always direct (on someone's income), and can sometimes be indirect, meaning they act as an increase on a good or service's price. An indirect tax is usually placed to dis-incentivise people from consuming/using a good or service. Just recently, Italy has announced the new tax it will be placing on plastic and sugar drinks from July 2020. This blog will be explaining about the details of the tax, and its impacts on the economy. Hope you like the blog!

This tax has already been placed in several other European countries, such as: the UK, France and Norway. The aim of this tax is to tackle several health issues such as: obesity and diabetes. The tax will be placed on fizzy-drinks (non-alcoholic) and fruit juices that have sugar and sweeteners. The government also plans to raise its revenue with this scheme. It will be directed not only towards consumers, but also towards producers, as the scheme also aims to contribute towards solving environmental issues.

The firms will be taxed €1 for every kilogram of plastic they produce. Bottle (or plastic-packaging) definitely requires the production of lots of plastic, which is responsible for environmental damage such as: killing several animals, and increasing volume of un-recyclable trash around the world. This tax may seem small, but still can affect several producers hugely. For example, a company named 'Sibeg' which produces bottles for Coca-Cola (located in Sicily), is estimated to see a revenue loss (income generated from sales) of €84 million (27%), and see a profit (revenue – cost) reduction of €16.7 million. The tax will also force producers to shift from plastic-packaging to non-plastic or reusable packaging.

Italy can potentially become a healthier country if the tax works well. As stated before, the health issues this tax hopes to solve are: obesity and diabetes. Although these drinks alone don't contribute to obesity and diabetes, they hugely increase the chances of getting these health issues. A tax on these drinks will lead to a decline in their consumption and reduce the prevalence of obesity and diabetes in the country. A healthier population potentially leads to economic growth, since the population can work better without facing any problems, and this can contribute to increasing output of the country.

The government estimates that this new tax will lead to their revenue increasing by €1.3 billion (US$1.45 billion). Currently the government is facing a budget deficit, since it is spending more (€870.8 billion), than it is receiving (€823.76 billion). Overall, it has a budget deficit of €47.04 billion. Although the revenue increasing seems insignificant, in the long-term it can help the government's budget deficit to plummet.

Overall, it is anticipated that this new scheme will lead to both benefits and costs to different parties. The Parties benefitting from the tax are: the government, since they can narrow the gap between their spending and revenue. The consumers, since they can potentially enjoy a healthier lifestyle, and the environment as a whole, since plastic production can see a huge drop. This scheme will leave producers of these soft-drinks with huge losses, due to reduced revenue. In my opinion, this is a good scheme, since, it generally benefits more people, and it can work towards economic growth.

Anyways, thanks for reading this blog! Hope you liked it!

ePrabhavnomics blog 65
Originally Published on: 1 December 2019

France plans to place taxes on flights

As mentioned in several of my blogs, air travel is a major source of air pollution. And as you all know air pollution negatively affects people's health, sometimes also leading to death. Therefore, we can assume that if air travel reduces, the amount of air pollution can reduce as well. Recently, France has decided to place a tax on flights leaving the country. This blog will be exploring the amount of the taxes, and how they will impact France. PS: France is still planning to implement this, so this blog will be talking about possible effects. Hope you like it!

So the taxes placed are as follows; for economy flights flying within the EU will be taxed €1.50. For economy flights flying outside the EU the tax will be €3. The tax for business flights within the EU will €9, and for business flights outside the EU the tax will be €18. The tax will be same for every airline company, and will be valid from any French airport. With this tax France expects to raise around €180 million from 2020.

Few people claimed that, according to them the tax rate of €18 was still too low. As that number didn't fully represent the amount of air pollution which flights were causing. And even said that the tax rates should be placed according to the amount of kerosene (the fuel used in airplanes, is also used in households at times). Since, two flights flying outside the EU (one to Morocco and the other to Thailand), will use different levels of kerosene.

In my opinion (rest of the blog is my opinion), these taxes may lead to a decline in number of flights leaving France, however the fall may not be significant, since few people may need to use airplanes for several different reasons, for example, business meetings. In such cases (business meetings), the passengers won't be able to avoid air travel. However it could potentially reduce voluntary air travel, such as air travel for holidays. However, I could also argue that some people, who want to visit places they have never visited may still travel by airplanes without caring about the price increase.

The extra €180 million can be used to develop infrastructure of less polluting transportation, for example, trains, hybrid cars. The government can work on increasing railway network, possibly even to other countries bordering France. This way the passengers will be able to use trains rather than planes when travelling to nearby countries. The extra revenue can be used to increase production of hybrid cars. Hybrid cars generally pollute much less than diesel cars, therefore an increased quantity of them on the streets will reduce the chances of steep pollution increase. These changes in infrastructure may or may not affect the number of flights taken every year, however I believe it is always important to take steps to reduce a problem.

Overall, placing tax can is a good initiative, even though I did say that in my opinion it will lead to a minor decline in air travel, it is a good starting point, and the tax can be increased over the years.

After a certain point, the effect of the tax will be significant on the passengers, and will lead to a huge drop in air travel. However, the government should also work on improving the infrastructure and availability of less polluting transportation, this way the commuters will have an option when flight tickets are very priced.

Hope you liked this blog! Thanks for reading!

What is your opinion on this topic?

ePrabhavnomics blog 66
Originally Published on: 8 December 2019

Factors leading to economic growth

In several of my blogs I have used the term 'economic growth' and how one factor will lead to 'economic growth'. However, have any of you wondered what exactly factors to economic growth, and what don't? Well in this blog I will be explaining all the factors that will contribute to economic growth. Before starting I would just like to clarify that, economic growth is defined as, 'an increase in the production of goods and services over a period of time, usually a year'. Now that we have this clarified let's get started. Hope you like this blog!

First we have 'accumulation of capital'. Accumulation of capital is defined as, 'a business purchasing more capital stock (number of shares a company has), which can later be used to produce goods.' This action can also be called, 'investment'. It leads to economic growth because, when firms buy the capital stock they add money to the economy. Similarly, with greater capital they can produce more goods, and the sellers of the capital stock can produce more capital, both of which lead to an economic growth.

Apart from just investment, an increase in overall demand for goods and services in an economy will lead to economic growth. The total demand (aggregate demand – AD) for an economy is calculated using the formula; Consumption (C) + Investment (I) + Government Spending (G) + (Export – Imports) (X-M). I have already written a blog on this topic in more detail (blog 23). Anyways, an increase in any of these factors leads to an increase in the amount of cash in the economy, this incentivises producers to increase production of goods and services. You may have noticed I put, 'Exports – Imports', the reason for this is, when you export goods you are given cash in-return for them, which later adds on to the economy. Conversely with imports, you spend in another country when buying the goods, imports therefore helps the other countries' economy. So in conclusion, X-M, represents the difference between money received from trades, and spend in trades.

Increases in labour supply. Usually goods and services are produced by workers, therefore if there are greater number of workers the chances of an increased production also increases. Not just sheer number of workers, but also worker productivity (amount of goods/services produced in a given amount of time) is very important. This is because, fewer workers with higher worker productivity can produce more compared to more workers with low worker productivity. It is also possible that the working hours are increased, which raises the possibilities of increased production.

Technological advancements. An example of a technological advancement includes, better machinery. Better machinery includes, machinery that is able to produce goods faster, or of better quality. More goods produced leads to economic growth. If better quality goods are produced, the demand for these goods rises, and as discussed before greater demand leads to an economic growth. However, on the flip side, better technology will mean less workers are required in the workforce, which will lead to rise in unemployment. Unemployment in general is a negative for the economy, also the unemployed won't be able to purchase as many goods and services as before, leading to a dip in the AD, and slowing down economic growth.

Overall, these were the factors that help lead to economic growth. As you may have noticed, all these factors lead to an increased number of goods and services in the economy. And this is key to achieving economic growth, the economy must produce more goods and services. We also saw that one of these points, 'technological advancements' had a con, which led to economic decline. Therefore it is important to also look at the other side of the coin when deciding whether a certain factor will really lead to a certain result.

Anyways, hope you liked the blog! Thanks for reading!

ePrabhavnomics blog 67
Originally Published on: 15 December 2019

Factors affecting consumption in an economy

Consumption is the act of normal citizens buying goods and services. Consumption is an important factor that leads to economic growth of a country. Higher the consumption, more economic growth will take place. The main reason for this is because, when people spend they add money in the economy, which can later be used to increase production in the economy. This blog will be looking at the factors which can lead to an increase in consumption. Hope you like this blog!

First is, amount of disposable income available. Disposable income is the income available after taxation. Usually, when disposable income is higher people tend to spend more. However, we can also consider 'discretionary income', when determining how much the consumers have left to spend. Discretionary income also subtracts the necessary bills from the total income. The necessary bill includes: rent, mortgage, food, education, property maintenance. In short, the amounts covered in the 'necessary bills' includes all the costs required to survive. Overall, while disposable income takes into account income available for necessities and luxuries, discretionary income only looks at income left for luxuries. Both are good, however for spending in the economy, knowing disposable income is better, since spending on both necessities and luxuries is calculated.

If we divide goods into two categories, necessities and luxuries. Luxuries are goods which people don't generally need, but prefer to have them, such as, more expensive cars. Meanwhile necessities are goods which are required for survival of people, such as, food and water. If incomes drop, demand for necessities won't fall as much, meanwhile with luxuries the demand fro them will drop significantly. Therefore, depending on the number of necessities and luxuries in the country, we can determine how much the consumption will drop, depending on the fall in income.

Phase on the business cycle. The business cycle is an economic model that shows how gross domestic product (GDP) will change overtime. Whenever the business cycle is in the 'recession phase' the phase when GDP growth is negative, there is usually a fall in employment. This is mainly because, when the economy is shrinking, fall in income leads to drop in demand, so workers are laid-off, so that firms don't face losses. Due to fall in income, and possible risk of unemployment (it is not necessary that firms lay workers off), consumer decide it is better to save up rather than consume. On the other hand, when the economy is growing, consumption rises, for the opposite reasons.

Price levels. Usually, when price levels are low people tend to increase consumption. Therefore, when there are lower prices the economy can grow faster. However, we can again divide goods into two categories; luxuries, and necessities. When price levels are high, consumption of luxuries might reach a level low, however consumption of necessities may remain stagnant. Therefore, the number of necessities and luxuries is important in determining how the prices levels will affect overall consumption in the economy. Higher prices will lead to lower consumption overall, but if more necessities are present in the economy, the drop might not be too significant.

Overall, the factors that affect consumption in an economy are; amount of disposable income, phase on the business cycle and price levels. For, income and price, the levels of consumption depend of whether the good is a necessity or a luxury. Meanwhile, for a recession in the economy, luxuries will definitely see a huge fall, and possibly, if income levels see a huge dip, the consumption of necessities might also see a significant fall, mainly due to lack of purchasing power.

Hope you liked this blog! Thanks for reading!

ePrabhavnomics blog 68
Originally Published on: 22 December 2019

Factors affecting trade balance of an economy

Trade is the act of firms buying/selling goods from/to foreign firms, and as mentioned in several of my blogs, trade is one of the factors that can lead to economic growth. When number of exports, are greater than the number of imports, the economy can see a growth. This is because, when more is exported, more money is received by firms, than spent (on imports). There are lots of factors that lead to an increase in the quantity of trade taking place in an economy. This blog will be explaining these factors, so hope you like it!

First factor is; trade restrictions. There are two types of trade restrictions, which a government can impose, they are, tariffs and quotas. Tariffs are extra prices placed on goods, meanwhile quotas are when there is a limit placed on the number of goods that can be imported to a country over a period of time (usually an year). Both these methods reduce the number of imports a certain country receives. Unless the good with the tax is an absolute necessity for the foreign country, the amount of that good that is exported won't significantly drop. In case you are wondering why trade restrictions will be imposed in the first place, you can read my blog 48.

Demand for that particular good. Higher the demand for a particular good, more of that good is exported. If a country is in dire need of a particular good, but due to different reasons isn't able to produce that good, they may ask other countries to export it to their country. If more of that good is required, more of that good will be traded. Greater demand can also help the exporting country increase production of that good, subsequently leading to that country seeing an economic growth. The country that is able to acquire high demand for most of its goods will see the greatest economic growth.

Exchange rates. When buying foreign goods, the firms will look at the exchange rate in order to find out how much they have to pay for buying the good. Since lower prices attract more people, the lower the exchange rates, more people will buy their goods. When the exchange rates appreciates (goes up), the firm can expect to sell less to foreign companies, since their goods will seem dearer for foreigners, (opposite is true for a depreciation in the exchange rate). In case you didn't understand how, here is a short explanation, if €1=Indian rupees 80, and Indian firms sell a good to Italy for Indian rupees 100K, Italian firm has to pay €1.25K. Now if the exchange rate falls to €1=Indian rupees 85, Italy will only have to pay (saying price of good is the same), €1.18K (so a lower price). India on the other hand will have to pay more for buying Italian goods. Overall, countries with lower exchange rates, will manage to export more and import less, (as mentioned why in the intro), which will lead to an economic growth.

Inflation. Inflation is when a country sees an increase in price levels. Due to inflation, it is possible that even with low exchange rates, a particular country sees low demand from foreign firms, since its goods have very high prices. It is possible that a country facing high inflation might purchase more goods from overseas. Since domestic goods are unaffordable, or firms don't have enough revenue to buy costlier raw material. This will lead to the country seeing more imports, and lower exports, which means the country doesn't see a significant economic growth (all factors remaining equal).

Overall, these were the factors that will affect the amount of trade taking place in an economy. So, these factors include; trade restrictions, demand, exchange rates and inflation. In order for a country to be able to export more, it need to face no trade restrictions, needs high demand from foreigners, needs to have a low exchange rates and low inflation. With all of these, the country can see a significant rise in exports, ultimately leading to a drastic increase in GDP.

Hope you liked this blog! Thanks for reading!

ePrabhavnomics blog 69
Originally Published on: 29 December 2019

Major economic events that took place in 2019

2019 is coming to an end, and we are about to enter not only a new year but also a new decade. This being my final blog of 2019, I will list down the major economic events that have taken place this year. This list contains only the events which I believe were important. So, if you think I missed out an event which according to you was significant, definitely let me know. Hope you like this blog! PS: At the start of the year, I wrote a blog on what was expected to take place this year (blog 18), so you can compare these two blogs to see if what was expected to happen has occurred or not.

New Brexit deal announced. After several deadline shifts, from 29 March 2019 to 31 October 2019, to (now) 31 January 2020, there have been several changes in the Brexit deals. This year (in July) after Parliament rejected Mrs May's Brexit deal, and she resigned as Prime Minister (PM), Mr (Boris) Johnson took over as PM and some changes in the Brexit deal. Johnson created a custom and regulatory border (inspection of goods at borders before they enter the country) between Northern Ireland and Great Britain. He however kept few things unchanged, such as; the rights of UK citizens in EU and of EU citizens in UK. On 20 December 2019, in Parliament this bill got a majority of 124 (358 for, 234 against). This bill will now go through further examination in Parliament. It is to be seen what the future of Brexit will be.

India General Elections. There were several countries that held their general elections in 2019, for example UK (12 December 2019). However, I consider India's elections 2019 as an important event because, the winner was 'Narendra Modi' and, as explained in my blog 38, I believe that he has helped India develop in a very positive way. With him winning, we can expect India to see more progress, in the coming years. Wishing him and his team the best of luck.

Also relating to India, Article 370 and 35A were scrapped, meaning now Kashmir no longer has the rights to have a separate constitution. Kashmir will now have to abide by the Constitution of India, and now Kashmir has shifted from a state to two Union Territories; Jammu & Kashmir and Ladakh. Since Kashmir is now part of the India's Constitution, we can now hope for more peace in the Kashmir valley.

There were several protests that took place on the streets this year. Mostly because the citizens were unhappy with the government. Examples of countries with these protests are; Hong Kong, Iraq, Lebanon, Algeria and France (yellow vests – also took place last year). This isn't the first year when anti-government protests have taken place, however this year saw a significantly huge number of protests taking place and that too across the globe. Therefore it is a massive concern that a considerably large number of countries are not satisfied with their governments, and I hope the government responds to the citizens' pleas.

Fridays For Future (FFF) protests. These protest are done by school students, who skip school (on Fridays) to demonstrate for a climate action, to prevent increases in global warming and more extreme climate change. It was first organised by a Swedish 15 year old girl (Greta Thunberg), who in August 2018 protested outside the Swedish Parliament. Post this, few countries saw some climate protest on their streets, however 15 March 2019 marked the first global protest, with more than 125 countries participating in it. This year has seen many climate strikes. I believe it is important that our voice is heard to the government (as well as contributing to the change too), since we need to save the planet or the future, no matter what happens to the economy.

Overall, these were few of the events that took place in this year which I believe were the most important. If you think I have missed out any event which you believe was crucial, please let me know. Anyways, hope you had a lovely 2019. Wishing you all, all the best for 2020. There are many economic and non-economic events expected to take place in 2020, which I will be talking about in my next blog! Thanks for reading! Hope you liked this blog!

ePrabhavnomics blog 70
Originally Published on: 5 January 2020

Major events expected to take place in 2020

2020 has begun, and just like every year, this year is also expected to have many significant events taking place. In this blog I will be talking about some events that are expected to take place in 2020. This list obviously won't contain every single event that will take place in 2020, mainly because some sudden events could take place, and few ones could be delayed and will instead take place in 2021. Before starting this blog, I would like to wish everyone a Happy New Year!

First on my list is Brexit, which is expected to take place on 31 January. After changing dates several times in 2019, it has been agreed (as of now) that the UK will leave European Union (EU) on 31 January 2020. After the UK leaves the EU, it will immediately enter a 'transition period' until 31 December 2020. During the transition period the UK will have to follow the EU rules and its trading relationship with other EU countries will remain the same, also the UK will continue to contribute to the EU's budget. All of this will end after the transition period ends.

Next on the list is the Tokyo Olympics. The Tokyo Olympics is expected to take place between 24 July and 9 August. It will host over 200 nations, with over 10,000 athletes and around 300 events in 33 sports. I personally believe the Olympics are important because, it gives the athletes an opportunity to represent their country internationally, and they can show their skills to the world. The success story of different athletes that worked hard to win at the olympics can inspire several people to work harder to achieve their dreams.

Dubai Expo. The Dubai Expo is expected to start on 20 October, and will continue till 10 April 2021. The Expo in my opinion is a significant event because, it allows people to share their country's culture to the rest of the world. Every Expo has a different universal theme, for example last Expo (Milan 2015), had the theme of "Feeding the Planet, Energy for Life". Dubai Expo's theme will be "Connecting Minds, Creating the Future". The Dubai Expo with this theme aims to inspire the future generation to increasing their creativity and to think in a more innovative way, so that the world can make lots of progress in the future decades.

Both the Tokyo Olympics and the Dubai Expo can help both the economy of Japan and United Arab Emirates to grow. This is because, both places will see a huge inflow of tourists. One of the reasons being, tourists will have to pay for lodging, food amongst many other things. The amount paid by the tourists gets added to the total value of the economy. I have written a complete blog on how tourism effects the economy (blog 22).

The United States presidential elections. On 3 November the US will see its 59th quadrennial (occurring every 4 years) presidential election. On 14 December the members of the Electoral College (a body of electors which have been decided by the US Constitution, that play the role of electing the President and Vice President of the US), will meet in their respective state capital cities to formally decide the President and Vice President. Then, on 20 January 2021, there will be an inauguration ceremony (if the current President isn't re-elected). Back in 2016 (previous presidential election), lots of people were unhappy with the results of the elections, therefore it will be interesting to see whether the Americans repeat their same 'mistake' even this time or not.

Overall, these were some of the incidents which are expected to take place in 2020, which I believe are important. If any of you thinks that I have missed any important event, please let me know. Thanks for reading! Hope you liked the blog!

<u>ePrabhavnomics blog 71</u>
Originally Published on: 12 January 2020

Effects of education and passing exams on the economy

Everyone has taken exams during their school lives. Nobody likes taking them, but unfortunately they are necessary in helping decide our future (most times). Doing better in exams can increase your chances of gaining a higher status in life (again most times). Also, having more people that did better in exams (more educated people), can help the economy in many ways. This blog will be looking at how having more educated people in a country can help boost the economy. Hope you like this blog!

Higher employment rate. Many jobs require certain skills, qualifications from the workers. In order to acquire these skills, qualifications the people need to go through some sort of education. Without any education, it will be difficult for them to get these skills, since schools/universities teach many of them. So, if less people have gotten formal education, less people will be employed.

Apart from just finding employment, you will get higher incomes. Higher your qualification, higher your income. This is because, lot more hard work is required to get a job requiring lots of skills, therefore income is higher for people with those jobs. Meanwhile, anyone is able to get a job requiring little to no qualifications, therefore income for those jobs is low. Higher income levels means better standard of living for the people, since with higher salaries they will find it easier to afford necessities and luxuries. Higher income usually leads to a rise in overall consumption in an economy. Higher consumption increase a country's aggregate demand (total demand for all goods and services), which causes economic growth. Therefore in conclusion, being more educated increases your chances of finding a job, and also of getting a huge salary.

Higher output from the economy. As discussed before, if more people are educated, more people will be employed (a firm may refuse to employ a worker that doesn't meet their required minimum qualifications). Therefore, a higher percentage of the workforce will be contributing to the output of the economy, therefore overall output of the economy will rise. Greater output means, the value of goods and services in the country is higher, therefore it will lead to a rise in the population's incomes (total output divided by total population is average income).

Another thing that needs to be taken into account while analysing education's effects on the economy is; the quality of education. Usually, more developed countries have better quality education. Quality education is when the students are able to gain experiences from schools/universities in order to become more productive in the working world. The environment in which the children learn should be, safe, lively and should be able to stimulate the students to learn. If these criteria are met, students will have a better time during their education, and can help them possibly do better in their careers. This is because, if there are several problems, the teacher may have difficulty teaching or students might have difficulty in learning. Therefore quality education is also important, and it heavily influences qualifications and skills received by the population.

Overall, these were few of the points that show the effects education has on the economy. Overall, education allows more people to participate in the workforce, which allows the economy to grow, and its also helps the population earn a higher income. The economy doesn't face any negative effects due to higher education. Therefore, more education is always a benefit for the economy. Hope you liked this blog! Thanks for reading!

ePrabhavnomics blog 72
Originally Published on: 19 January 2020

New trade deal between US and China

You may have heard about the ongoing trade war between the United States (US) and China. This trade war started on 22 January 2018, and has always had new trade restrictions announced from both sides (for example, higher tariffs). Recently (15 January), there was a new deal signed by both parties, and this time this new deal could put a pause on this conflict. This blog will be looking at what this pact says, and what are the effects of this pact. So, hope you like this blog!

This deal's main purpose is to finish the 'first chapter' of the trade war. In case anyone is wondering what I mean by first chapter (or

Phase One), I will briefly explain that there were some targets placed by US and China. Due to this pact, Phase One of this trade war has come to an end. China has committed itself to buying $200 billion worth of US goods and services by 2021. The breakdown of these $200 billion is: $52.4 billion of energy exports, $32 billion of agricultural products, $77.7 billion of manufactured goods and $37.9 billion of services. The US president believes that this new pact can be a boon for US farmers, who were the most affected (negatively) by the trade war. China on the other hand is relaxing the trade barriers which US goods have to face. There still are several things which this deal doesn't address, including some factors which hugely contribute to increase tension between the two countries (which will turn out to be a drawback of this agreement).

Despite this trade agreement not including a solution to everything that is causing a rift between the two countries, can provide several benefits to both economies. Like, due to China's lower trade barriers in food and agriculture, many US farmers will be able to export more goods to China, apart from the fact that China has already committed itself to buying $32 billion of agricultural products from the US, lower tariff barriers always makes it easier for a country to export its goods to another one. Both the economies have also agreed to not devalue their currencies, and have promised to publicly announce their foreign exchange reserves. This will help stop any of the two countries from gaining any export advantage.

Overall, this new deal could allow the global economy to grow faster. This trade war has impeded US and China from hugely trading with each other. Due to lower exports, the US economy and the Chinese economy have seen a lower growth rate. Due to this trade war seeing a pause, the two economies will see a higher number of exports. According to the International Monetary Fund (IMF), this conflict resulted in a loss of 0.8% of the global gross domestic product (GDP) – around $700 billion.

This deal still has drawbacks. Since the deal leaves some of the conflicts' major sources untouched, such as, China's approach to subsiding businesses. What this means is that China's government is financing companies, in order to help them increase productivity. The US believes that due to this it will lead to overcapacity (supply is higher than demand) and it will give then an unfair advantage in global markets. Therefore, China can go ahead of the US in terms of trading. According to this agreement, the US has still kept the $360 billion of tariff on Chinese goods, which is highest tax Americans have to pay, compared to when buying from elsewhere. These issues may need a 'Phase 2' deal to be solved, which seems unlikely for the time being. Until the Phase 2 deal isn't signed, many US firms won't buy many goods from China, and China will continue to export its goods elsewhere. This will lead to no progress between the two economies.

So in conclusion, this was my blog on the new trade deal between US and China. This new trade deal can help both economies buy more goods from each other, and can possibly help the global economy to grow faster. But, since this new deal isn't addressing everything it can still lead to there being no progress in the relationship between US and China. The US president might come up with a Phase 2 deal in November (post the elections), however we also don't know the results of the election, and possibly from now to then the situation may get worse, since both US and China can decide to not buy each other's goods. All the consequences remain to be seen, let's hope for the best in the meantime.

Hope you liked this blog! Thanks for reading!

ePrabhavnomics blog 73
Originally Published on: 26 January 2020

How did India become a republic?

Today (26 January) is Indian republic day. On this day in 1950, India was no longer ruled by the kings and queens, and the Indian constitution (government) was formed. This was roughly 2 and a half years post India's Independence from the British, on 15 August 1947. But what was the process with which India become a republic post? This blog will be looking at what the process that took place to make India a republic. So, hope you like this blog! And wishing you all Indians a happy republic day. PS: I honestly feel republics are better than monarchies (ruled by kings), so I feel India was better after being a republic. I have already written a blog on the differences between republics and monarchies (blog 33).

Before looking at the journey India took to become a republic, let's look at how India was governed between 1947 and 1950. When India gained Independence, it didn't have a constitution, India's law was based on the 'Government of India Act 1935'. The Government of India Act 1935, was a Parliamentary Act passed in the Parliament of UK in August 1935. This act ended the dyarchy (government by two independent authorities), which was introduced in the 'Government of India Act 1919', it also provided for a set-up of a 'Federation of India'. The Federation of India was supposed to be made of provinces of British India and some Princely states. But the required number of princely states didn't join, due to which the Federation wasn't formed. Until India's republic day, India's ruler was King George VI.

Looking at India's journey to becoming a republic. The first step was taken by Nehru (a politician at that time – became 1st Prime Minister of India in 1947) in Lahore at the Indian National Congress (INC) conference on 31 December 1929. All the nationalists at the conference vowed to mark 26 January as the country's Independence Day from the British. This conference also helped to give birth to the 'Civil Disobedience Movement' (non-violent protests for Independence). It was made certain 26 January 1930 be marked as the day of complete Independence. The dream of India's Independence begun from that instance.

In the meantime, Gandhi started the protests for Independent India on 12 March 1930. On that day, he along with 78 followers, conducted a march to the coastal town of Dandi on the Arabian Sea. This movement of his made students leave colleges, and government servants resigned from offices. Apart from this there was a huge burning down of foreign clothes and people decided to stop paying government taxes.

The Indian Constituent Assembly, which was formed due to negotiations between Indian leaders and members of the British

Cabinet Mission (a group which came to India, with the goal of discussing the transfer of power from the British government to leadership of India), had their first meeting on 9 December 1946. The aim of the Indian Constituent Assembly was to write India's constitution, which could be used for a long period of time. A large number of committees were made in charge to research the contents of the proposed constitution. After many discussions and debates and revision on the proposed constitution, the Indian Constitution was finalised and legally accepted, on 26 November 1949.

Although India gained independence on 15 August 1947, the country enjoyed true independence from 26 January 1950, after the Constitution of India came into force. This new Constitution gave Indian people the power to rule themselves, by choosing their own government. Since then, this day is celebrated every year as India's republic day, giving the nation a national holiday.

So, this was my blog on India's journey to becoming a republic. Once again wishing you all Indians a very Happy Republic Day! Be Proud of your Nationality! Anyways, thanks for reading! Hope you liked this blog!

ePrabhavnomics blog 74
Originally Published on: 2 February 2020

What if the EU was never formed?

2 days ago (31 January), Brexit happened, which means the United Kingdom (UK) left the European Union (EU). This blog won't talk about Brexit, since I have already written two blog on it (blog 30 and 31), but I will be about the EU. For those who don't know, the EU is a 'political and economic union of 27 countries located in Europe.' Due to the EU's formation, its members have benefitted and also faced many disadvantages. This blog will be analysing what would have happened if the EU wasn't formed. So hope you enjoy this blog!

First let's talk about the benefits the EU members would have received without the EU (EU's disadvantages). The first benefit is that the members can have their own policies. The EU has taken away the rights from governments of individual countries to create their own policies, and have to follow the EU's policies. This is a disadvantage for countries who don't agree with certain policies of the EU, for different reasons. So in conclusion we can say without the EU, the countries will have more freedom in policy making.

No 'single currency' problems. As you may know every EU member has a single currency, which is 'the Euro'. This is a disadvantage for EU members because, since every country is facing different economic problems. For example, if a country is facing higher inflation than other countries, it might need to raise its interest rates (to reduce borrowing from banks). Even if all countries won't be facing the same problems at a given time, since all the countries have a single currency, they are obliged to comply with any changes to the monetary policy (actions done by the central bank to manage money supply). So, using this example, every country (with the euro) will be forced to raise interest rates, and this can be negative for other countries, that might need low interest rates. So in conclusion, without a single currency, every country will have its own monetary policy and can change it according to their own needs, without hampering any other country's economy.

Now lets move on to the costs which the countries will have to face without the EU (EU's advantages). The first costs is that members will have to face tariffs (taxes) when trading to other members. The EU is considered as a 'trade bloc'. So this means the countries can trade goods and services with each other without facing any costs. This is a benefit for all EU members since, they can increase their exports. More exports leads to an economic growth, since exporting increases cash going inside a particular country. Now if the EU didn't exist, it is possible that the countries may have trade tariffs amongst each other, this reduces the amount of exports they can make, since trading to those countries will become more expensive and therefore can limit economic growth.

Fall in tourism. Travelling to EU countries from a EU country is not very expensive, since visa is not required. Without the EU, visa might be required when doing such sorts of travel, thus raising travelling costs. Higher travelling costs will possibly reduce number of tourists going to a particular destination. Countries will see a decline in the tourism industry due to fewer tourists, and this can lead to a slowdown in economic growth. Tourists lead to economic growth, because, when they spend in a foreign country, that money goes into the total economy. When it comes to tourism, the lack of a single currency can prove to be a disadvantage for the EU members. Right now, tourists are finding it easier to travel since they don't have to exchange currencies. Having to exchange currencies may prove to be a hassle for some tourists, and they may decide to not go abroad. This again leads to a fall in a country's tourism.

Fewer jobs available and possibly worse working conditions. A lot of the jobs in EU countries are directly linked to the EU. This means that people are employed in the 'Institution of the EU', like the 'European Parliament'. Without the EU, all these people will lose their jobs, leading to mass unemployment. Apart from this, the EU has some specific rules that protect workers' rights (named as 'Working Time Directive'). Some rules include weekly work should exceed an average of 48 hours, or those working more than 6 hours (a day) are entitled for a break. Without the EU and these rules, some workers may go through worse working conditions.

Overall, the countries will face more disadvantages than advantages if the EU didn't exist. Therefore it is a good thing that the EU was formed. Anyways, hope you liked this blog! Thanks for reading!

ePrabhavnomics blog 75
Originally Published on: 9 February 2020

Completion of 75 blogs – History of my blogs

Hello everyone, today I am posting my 75th consecutive blog. On this occasion I won't be writing about a different topic, but instead I will be writing about few of my blogs which I will chose randomly. So, hope you like this blog! And thank you all for supporting me for the past 75 weeks.

I will start by talking about my first blog, in which I wrote about what would happen if 1US$ was equal to 1 Indian rupees. I spoke about how due to this, India will see a rise in its imports, as they will be cheaper for Indian firms to buy. But on the contrary, foreign firms will find Indian exports more dearer to buy, so exports will fall. And India will also see an increase in labour cost, so unemployment in the country will rise.

Fast forward to blogs 30 and 31, I wrote about something that recently occurred, Brexit. Blog 30 was about how UK will be impacted due to Brexit. I wrote about how UK will find it harder to export to other EU countries, as the other EU countries can place tariffs (taxes) on UK exports. Also, UK's economic growth will fall, as firms will cut investment, due to uncertainty about the future. The slower growing economy will also cause many other negative impacts, like fall in employment in the UK. Blog 31 was about how the EU will be impacted from Brexit. The EU will see a huge drop in its budget, as UK contributes to around 12% of the EU's budget. EU will see a huge drop in export money received, this is because the UK was the EU's largest exporter (contributing to 22% of the EU's exports).

Later I wrote about which countries are predicted to have the largest economies in 2030 (blog 55). The top 5 largest economies in 2030 are expected to be: 1) China 2) India 3)US 4) Indonesia and 5) Turkey. The current developing countries will grow faster than the developed countries, and will contribute to a larger percentage of total growth in the upcoming decade, than developed countries. A major reason for this trend is the closing gap between rich and poor, and many developing countries getting hold of the resources developed countries already have.

In one of my recent blogs I wrote about the benefits an economy can have if extra 'walking' took place in the economy, (blog 63). I spoke about how more walking makes people healthier. If people are healthier, they will be able to produce more in the economy. Healthier means they can live for longer and also possibly work for longer, if older people work for longer the economy can see an increase in the working population. A higher working population usually means more workers can contribute to output of the economy.

In my last week's blog (blog 74), I wrote about what would happen if the EU never existed? It can be seen that the EU countries would face more disadvantages, than advantages without the EU. Therefore, it is a good thing that the EU was formed. Disadvantages the countries would have to face include: higher travel costs and possible tariffs reduce trade between countries. The advantages were: countries can create their own policies and no 'single currency' problems.

So this was the summary of few of my past blogs! Hope you liked this blog! Hope you all support me till I reach to 100 blogs! Thanks for reading!

ePrabhavnomics blog 76
Originally Published on: 16 February 2020

Impacts of an epidemic on the economy

Recently, in China there was the outbreak of the 'coronavirus'. As of now the virus seen around 45,000 cases in over 20 countries (most of them are from China). An epidemic is defined as, 'the spreading of a disease in an area over a particular time period'. The coronavirus is considered as an epidemic, since it is rapidly spreading and is affecting people from many countries (starting from only China). This epidemic has lead to several things like, many people changing their behaviour towards China. This blog will be analysing the effects of epidemics on the economy. So hope you like this blog!

The first impact is: fewer exports bought. As the coronavirus started in China, may foreigners (consumers and firms), have started avoiding Chinese goods and services in fear of getting infected. This can be the case with any country which sees the outbreak of a virus. When less goods and services of a country are bought, the country sees a drop in economic growth. This is because, the demand for that country's goods is lower, so cash received by the country also falls.

Like in China, it is possible that some factories (of a country facing an epidemic) may decide to shut down for a while, just so to avoid interaction between workers, which can lead to a spreading of the virus. A closing of factories will lead to a significant drop in the number of goods produced by the country, which will slow down the economy, or even make it decline. Apart from hurting the economy, it will also hurt the consumers. The consumers won't receive any income, as the factories are shut down. The people will therefore find it harder to pay for basic needs.

Drop in number of tourists going to the country. The number of international tourists arriving to the country will fall drastically after the virus, since obviously nobody is willing to catch it. A fall in tourism will affect the economy as a whole, since fewer cash inflows are entering the economy. And, it can also lead to a rise in unemployment, as less people will be needed to work in the tourist industry.

Strain on the government to invest in health care. Demand for health care might peak during such periods, as everyone is hoping to stay safe from the virus. Due to very high demand, the government will be forced to invest in health care, in order to help it get better. By doing this, the government has to forgo investing in other areas of the economy, which might be in need.

Harder to travel abroad. Due to this epidemic, many foreign countries may require visa, or other regulations which travellers (from the country of the epidemic) are forced to comply to, as foreigns are now scared that their nation may be infect with the virus. This is a cost, as the residents will now have to go through more obstacles when going abroad, something they could have done more easily, if not for the virus.

Overall these were the economic impacts of an epidemic. An economy can only face negative impacts from the outbreak of a virus, there never are any positive impacts. As seen in the blog, when there is an epidemic mainly, people avoid going to that country, and people from that country are faced with barriers which make it harder for them to go to other countries.

So hope you liked this blog! Thanks for reading!

ePrabhavnomics blog 77
Originally Published on: 23 February 2020

Why Italy's economy is doing better than many people think?

Italy is a 'more economically developed country' (MEDC). Just like other MEDCs in the world, Italy's economy is growing at a slow rate, but Italy's economic growth rate is much smaller than many of the other countries in the European Union (EU). Italy's economy is growing at a rate of around 0.5% annually, meanwhile most of the other EU countries are growing at rates of over 2% annually. Despite this stagnant growth, Italy's economy is actually doing better than what many people think, and this is what today's blog will be analysing. So, hope you like this blog!

First reason is: foreign investment. Italy is still receiving lots of foreign investment. The major reason for Italy still receiving abundant foreign investment is, its relatively low living costs and the huge return of investment (profit as a percentage of costs). One form of foreign investment is; buying real estate. Demand for real estate is on the rise in Italy, mainly because local people in Italy mainly prefer to live in their own house, and most Italian families are buying second homes for holidays. Italy is also seeing positive net migration (more people entering the country), so the migrants help to increase demand for estate. Also, rise in tourism to Italy is helping foreign investment grow. This is because, investors are buying property to help accommodate the tourists.

Next is: trade surplus. Trade balance is calculated by finding the different between exports and imports (exports – imports). If a country has more exports than imports, it has a trade surplus. Italy is the 7th largest exports in the world, and 3rd largest in Europe and it exports large quantities of many goods, which are crucial to foreign countries, like: machinery, pharmaceuticals, furniture and many more. This gives the country an opportunity to increase its production in these goods, and further increase its exports. The country's trade balance is expected to remain mostly positive for the following years, therefore it will continue to be a benefit for the country.

Small but efficient firms. Having lots of small firms isn't really something positive, as usually their production is low and there isn't a great opportunity at finding employment in small firms. However, since most of Italy's firms are 'small and medium sized', having a large number of small firms can prove an advantage to Italy. This is because, their won't be dominated by larger firms. One of the main benefits of small firms is that, they are able to adapt easily to better technology and new material, something which can be hard for large firms. This flexibility helps them improve productivity quickly.

Overall, these are the reasons that are helping the Italian economy perform better than what is projected. However, the economy is still facing many problems, like, ageing population, which is causing the workforce to go in decline. The problems, unfortunately, outweigh these points mentioned. Due to this reason the Italian economy is growing at a slow rate, and also growth is declining. These factors can't be relied on for long, and a solution needs to be found in order to solve the slow economic growth. But it is still a good news to know the economy isn't in such a serious concern.

Hope you liked this blog! Thanks for reading!

ePrabhavnomics

ePrabhavnomics blog 78
Originally Published on: 1 March 2020

Benefits EU's gig workers will receive from Vestager

A gig worker is defined as, 'workers who either: work in their own firm, work on online platforms or are temporary workers (employees who work only during a certain time period, based on the needs of the firms).' In short, gig workers are workers who usually work on their own or are 'self-employed'. Two examples of gig workers are: Uber Drivers and Pizza Delivery Workers. Recently, the European Union (EU)'s antitrust chief, Margrethe Vestager, expressed that she wants to help gig workers, so they can receive better pay and better working conditions. This blog will look at what Vestager is expressing, and their possible effects on gig workers. So hope you like this blog!

Let's start with what exactly Vestager said. Vestager would like to help the people in 'weak negotiating positions' (less power to influence deals), and spoke about the poor condition of workers in the gig economy. She would like the EU people help the workers in the gig economy to unite, because she believes, uniting when you are working individually is difficult. Something else which Vestager wishes to address is 'EU's tough cartel rules', (cartel is when businesses decided to work together (collude) instead of competing). This is because, theses cartel rules have led to these colluding companies facing fines of billions of euros. These same rules have prevented self-employed workers from uniting. The union of these self-employed workers could have helped them fight for higher pay.

Now we will be analysing the possible impacts, if Vestager's desires are successful. Currently, many freelancers have to wait for a long time to receive their pay. This is because, they have to manage their own cash flow, and it is possible many clients may take long time to pay. This is a problem for freelancers, especially when they have to wait for very long. It is possible that, Vestager might come up with a solution to solve this issue, so self-employed workers don't face this problem again.

A possible minimum wage can be set for gig workers. It is difficult to impose a minimum wage on such types of jobs, because, most of the time the income earned by the workers is decided by apps, this is the case with companies like 'Deliveroo' and 'UberEats'. Using these two examples, the worker's pay can be increased if they deliver more orders in a certain time period. While attempts at making this possible have taken place, for example Deliveroo has campaigned for a long time for these workers to get more profits, it was unsuccessful. It is quite unclear how these minimum wages can be imposed, it is possible Vestager might come up with a solution to this problem.

There can be some changes to these cartel rules. Vestager might lead to the cartel rules seeing a change, especially if she points out their negative effects (end of paragraph 2). If these cartel rules become less tough, they can allow the self-employed workers come together, and fight for better rights.

Overall, it is hard to predict what exactly will happen to the EU gig workers, since Vestager has just expressed concern for them, she hasn't yet announced a plan to help them. However, it is a positive sign that someone is wishing for self-employed workers to have equal rights as traditional workers. It is to be seen what she will do next, and if she will be successful or not.

Hope you liked this blog! Thanks for reading!

ePrabhavnomics blog 79
Originally Published on: 8 March 2020

Advantages and Disadvantages faced by gig workers

As discussed in my previous blog (blog 78), gig workers are workers that work independently, meaning, either in their own firm or on online platforms. In the last blog I spoke about how gig workers face many problems in their life, and how the European Union's antitrust chief, Vestager has decided to raise her voice in their support. While they do have to go through many difficulties, there are still some advantages of having them. This blog will talk about the advantages and disadvantages of gig workers in the economy, and which outweighs which, thus giving us a conclusion on whether gig workers are mainly beneficial to the economy, or not. So, hope you enjoy this blog!

The first advantage is that, workers can be more flexible. Since gig workers are working independently, they have the option to be more flexible with their work schedule, for example they can choose the hours they want to work. Gig workers can sometimes feel like working for less hours, and this is very possible for them, since they aren't working for anyone. Gig workers won't need to rush on projects, since they can decide when they want to finish the project. This unfortunately can't happen with traditional jobs, as they are forced to follow a certain work schedule (most times), and are given strict deadlines on when to finish a task.

Workers can enjoy more independence. As mentioned in the previous point, workers in the gig economy can finish a project when they want. This is a benefit for them, since they don't have any pressure in finishing it, and this can help them finish the task with better quality. Having a better quality project, can help their business grow and become more successful. While this can lead to laziness, and procrastination, the workers might try and remain proactive, and try to finish the task as quick as possible, since it will be a loss for them and their own business.

The work isn't monotonous. In traditional jobs, a worker might have to work and complete the same task everyday, with makes his experience at work quite boring. Meanwhile, for gig workers, their tasks/projects may require them to do something different all the time, this makes their task more exciting. While it is true that having to do many different tasks can be a burden for them, since they don't have a specific deadline, they can take their own time to finish the tasks, and be more creative with them.

Now let's move on to the disadvantages. The disadvantage is, irregular pay. Gig workers don't receive their pay as regularly as people in traditional jobs. This is because, gig workers are paid depending on when they make their deliveries (food deliveries) or provide their services to the public (taxi drivers). So, the longer the gap between two of their deliveries and/or services the longer they stay without any pay.

Still have to pay taxes and manage own expenses. Gig workers are still forced to pay taxes, which they themselves finance. Linking back to the previous point, due to irregular pay, paying taxes becomes a hard task for the gig workers. Gig workers also need to manage their own expenses.

Some gig workers many feel lonely. While some people may prefer to be lonely, due to different reasons, like less distraction for them. Being lonely isn't something which many people will like, and this is a hurdle which gig workers not wanting to be lonely will have to face.

Lastly, gig workers always need to develop their skills. Since, gig businesses don't have high barriers to entry (obstacles preventing new companies from entering an area of business), so it is quite easy for other businesses to take over a gig business. To avoid this workers will need to constantly develop their skills in order to help their business grow and stop other businesses from taking over.

Overall these were the advantages and disadvantages of working in the gig economy. Overall we can see that, while the gig economy does have some advantages over traditional jobs in some criteria, the disadvantages mainly outweigh the advantages, therefore making the gig economy less favourable to work in.

Hope you liked this blog! Thanks for reading!

ePrabhavnomics blog 80
Originally Published on: 15 March 2020

Impacts of a pandemic on the global economy

In the last few weeks the coronavirus has spread across many countries, and currently over 150 countries have reported over 150,000 cases, and around 5600 people have died from the virus, though around 73,000 have recovered. This virus however, has lead to the lockdown of many countries, this means people are not allowed to leave their homes, unless they have a valid reason. Since this disease is occurring at a global level it is called a 'pandemic', meanwhile an 'epidemic' is more region based, and its spread is less than that of a pandemic. I have already written a blog on effects of an epidemic (blog 76), and focused on one country in that blog, this blog will focus on the global economy. So, hope you like this blog!

Let's start with the negatives, (yes there are some hidden positives impacts of this pandemic). The first negative point is; shortage of supply. After the lockdown was announced people went to supermarkets to buy large quantities of all essentials, so that they could survive for a long period of time without having to leave the house. Unfortunately, the supply of these goods wasn't enough for everyone, so a portion of the population had to survive without these necessities. Also, the population finished the goods quickly, and found it harder to purchase them again.

Due to the absence of workers at work, the global economy can see a decline. With fewer workers coming to work means total output produced by the industry falls, and leads to an overall decline in goods and services produced. This is evident from the new predictions which were made on the economic growth of countries in 2020 (by the OECD Economic Outlook Report). For example, China was initially predicted to see a 5.7% economic growth, but after the virus the prediction dropped to 4.9%. The global economy initially expected to grow at 2.9%, now is expected to grow by 2.4%. Due to advanced technology, it is very much possible that many companies have the facilities to contact their workers online, and continue with their work. But, in my opinion online work is not as effective as traditional work.

Many businesses will lose revenue. Many restaurants might have to temporarily close down due to lack of customers, this leads to revenue received by the businesses to decline. Lower revenue might create difficulty for these businesses to purchase the material they need to produce their goods.

No wages for workers. This might not be true for every single company, but some companies which requires workers to be physically present at the site might not give workers their wages. Low paid workers will be the most affected by this lockdown, but overall it will lower standards of living for the entire (or at least a large portion of) the population.

Now let's see the positives. The first positive is; dip in greenhouse gas emissions. If less people leave their house, there will be less vehicles are on the street. Vehicular pollution is one of the largest contributors of greenhouse gas emissions, and less vehicles can help greenhouse gas emission to drastically drop. Many industries might be closed, and so, industrial pollution will also be quite low (another major contributor of carbon emissions). Global warming is a major issue the world is currently facing, and these few weeks at home can help the planet see a respite from greenhouse gas emissions. While the problem of global warming won't be completely solved, it can be solved to a certain extent.

The next positive is, people can learn new skills. People can use this time off work to their advantage to learn new skills which can possibly help them be better/more efficient at their job. Which can help the economy recover its short period of slow growth in very little time. Higher efficiency by workers can help them see a rise in wages, and improve their living standards.

Overall, these were the positives and negatives this pandemic (or even any pandemic) can give to the population. Undoubtedly there are way more negative than positives, but if the population realises the 2nd positive (chance to learn new skills), they will definitely have a much happier life after this virus has finished.

Hope you liked this blog! Thanks for reading! Stay safe! Don't try and be rebels by going outside!

ePrabhavnomics blog 81
Originally Published on: 22 March 2020

What the world economy might be like after the coronavirus ends

The coronavirus pandemic isn't anywhere near stopping, in fact in the past week, the number of cases and deaths has risen more steeply (quickly). More countries are now in quarantine, my previous blog (blog 80) explored the impacts of this quarantine on the world economy, and most of the impacts were negative, however there were some hidden positive impacts of this quarantine. This blog will be looking at what the world economy might be like after the quarantine by all countries comes to an end (unsure when), and people can restart normal lives. So hope you like this blog!

The world economy is not going to see a steep rise immediately. It will take some time for things to settle down before life fully gets back to normal. This is because, people will still need to regain trust before purchasing goods from countries that were badly infected, or even go to those countries as tourists. Tourism to a country, and exports by a country are two major components in helping that country's economy grow. While the country can see growth in other factors (for example, consumption by people), the regain in economic growth won't be a high as it was before (at least for a while after the virus ends).

Every country can see an increase in aggregate demand (AD). AD is the total demand for all goods and services in an economy over a period of time, it is calculated by adding: total consumption by people, investment by firms, government expenditure and difference between exports and imports. I already explained that exports will take some time to see a spike, but the other 3 factors will definitely see an increase. Especially since the people will have more freedom of movement, and may return to purchasing in large amounts. But, as mentioned previous, due to exports not rising, the economic growth won't be as high as before. It is however also possible that, due to lower income by many people and lower revenue by companies during the quarantine period, the AD might not see an immediate rise.

The owners of many companies may force the workers to work for more hours, so that they are able to recover the production they lost during the quarantine period. It is unclear whether the workers will see a wage increase, this is mainly because, the company owners didn't see a revenue increase during the quarantine period. Most of the revenue available to firms will be needed to buy raw material for the production. It is still uncertain about whether the owners will do this or not, but if it happens the workers will be in a difficult situation, as they might not be used to working this hard after a long period of no work, and most likely they won't see an increase in pay for extra work.

Air pollution and global warming will see a rapid rise again (most probably). After everyone is free to move, more vehicles will be on the streets, leading to an increase in carbon emissions. Similarly, if companies decided to force their workers to work more, the industrial pollution will increase, (bound to happen even if workers aren't forced to work more). Currently, there are fewer flights flying across the globe, due to this pandemic, but after the pandemic ends, aerial pollution will also starting rising again. So in conclusion, after the quarantine ends, air pollution might see unprecedented growth again. So, all we can hope for it that people take more precautionary measures to help control the rate of global warming.

Overall these were the few predictions I made about how the world will be like after this quarantine is over. The short term impacts are mainly negative, but after sometime everything can get back to normal. Unfortunately we are still not sure of when this quarantine will end. Till then stay safe, and don't leave the house if it is not necessary. And, hope you all liked this blog. Thanks for reading!

ePrabhavnomics blog 82
Originally Published on: 29 March 2020

What would the economy be like if the coronavirus happened in the early 2000s?

The coronavirus pandemic isn't showing any signs of ending. In fact some countries, like USA and many European countries have seen a speed up in the increase in number of daily cases. No matter which era this virus takes place, its symptoms and effects on the human body will be the same. However, the era can affect the world economy and people (without the virus), in a different way. This blog will be exploring the effects the virus would have on world economy, if it took place in the early 2000s. So, hope you like this blog!

It would be harder for the workers to contact their companies during the lockdown. Due to advanced technology today, the companies and their workers can easily communicate with each other and continue their work, from their homes (smart work), like normal. This allows workers to continue getting their pay, and companies can continue to make progress. In the early 2000s however, the technology wasn't that developed, due to this, it was harder for workers and companies to communicate and continue their work. Workers therefore won't earn their pay, and companies can't make progress.

Secondly, it would be harder to spread the news of the virus and its safety precautions. The news and social media is helping people get aware of the virus, and the safety precautions they should take to avoid its spread. In the 2000s without social media, it would have been harder for the government to share the safety precautions with the population. This could lead to number of infected people rising even faster than it is today, and this would make it harder for the government to stop the spread of the virus. And as discussed in one of my blogs (blog 80), a pandemic (mostly) poses negative effects to the global economy and people. And, the situation can get worse if the pandemic isn't stopped in time.

The school and university students will not get any classes during the quarantine. Right now, schools offer online classes to their students, so that they keep up-to-date with the school work, and they can get through the syllabus on time. Without sufficient technology (in the early 2000s) required to conduct online classes, students won't get the learning they should, during the quarantine period. This will be negative for them, since some time of their lives will be wasted in recovering what they missed. This affects the economy as a whole, as the number of people in the workforce (people available for work), decreases. This is because, when people are in universities and schools they won't be in the workforce, and at the same time there will still be people retiring, so in conclusion, size of workforce decreases.

People won't be able to talk to anyone outside their house. Due to social media platforms people are able to chat with their friends and family members (with whom they don't live), this wouldn't have been possible back in the early 2000s, when such technologies didn't exist. People weren't able to communicate with the outside world, and this could have lead to depression among many people. Depression can damage someone's mental and emotional health, like it can give you, headache, insomnia, increased chance of heart disease, to name a few. This will be a problem for the government, as after having to work hard on stopping the coronavirus from spreading, they have to work on curing depression.

So, this was my blog on what the world economy would be like if the coronavirus took place in the early 2000s. As you can see, the effects of this pandemic would have been more dire back then compared to now. Let's hope that the pandemic comes to an end soon, and allows normal life to restart. Till then, be safe everyone.

Thanks for reading! Hope you liked this blog!

ePrabhavnomics blog 83
Originally Published on: 5 April 2020

Events that took place during the first quarter of 2020

Hello everyone, we have just entered the second quarter of 2020. In this blog I will be analysing the events that took place during the first quarter (January to March) of 2020. This 3 months have seen a large quantity of important events taking place, comparable to how many take place in a year. The blog will only consider the events, I consider were the most important, and will be listed in chronological order. So, hope you like this blog!

The first event is the: bushfire in Australia. While they started in June 2019, they continued in 2020, and in March 2020, the situation came under control. The bushfire (a fire in a forest) has had several negative effects on the Australian economy, as well as people and animals. The total area burned was, 186,361 km^2. More than 9000 buildings were destroyed, which included 3500 homes. 34 people were killed in this wildfire, and an estimate one billion animals have been killed (many of which are now extinct). The bushfire led to an estimated carbon emissions of 306 million tonnes in the air. The cost of dealing with the bushfires exceeded A$4 billion.

The next one is the: Persian Gulf Crisis. The Persian Gulf Crisis is the conflict between the US and Iran. This crisis initially started in May 2019, but gained heat on 8 January 2020. On that day, the Islamic Revolutionary Guard Corps (IRGC), conducted missile attacks on two Iraqi bases housing US troops, in order to avenge the assassination of Soleimani (an Iranian major general working in the IRGC). This almost led to war between the two nations. A key incident that took place during this period of tension, was the shooting of the 'Ukraine International Airlines Flight 752', which was found in the province of Tehran, Iran. It was later found that, it was shot by an Iranian SA-15 surface-to-air missile. Despite the current coronavirus crisis, the tensions between the two countries hasn't been relaxed.

On 31 January, the UK left the EU (or Brexit took place). This issue started in June 2016, when 52% people from the UK voted to leave the EU, in March 2017, the British government formally announced its withdrawal from the EU and started the Brexit process. After that, the UK constantly changed their date of withdrawal from the EU, and on 31 January 2020 they finally left the EU. This was a significant event since, both the UK and the EU will be negatively affected by Brexit. For example, the EU will lose a large percentage of the total budget, and the UK's economy will slow down. My blogs 30 and 31 talk about this issue in more detail.

Lastly, we have the coronavirus pandemic. The coronavirus's first case was registered in December 2019 in Wuhan, China. After that this virus started spreading around the globe, and as of today

(5 April 2020), the world has over 1.2 million coronavirus cases reported, in over 200 countries and around 65600 deaths (though more people recovered – 252,000). The COVID-19 is now a global pandemic, with all the infect countries in lockdown. This pandemic has stopped many businesses, and is leading to a drop in the global economy. It is still unclear as to when this pandemic will come to an end, especially because many countries are still seeing a rapid increase in their number of cases. This pandemic has also led to the cancelling of the 2020 Summer Olympics, they will now take place in 2021.

In conclusion, these were the incidents that took place in the first quarter of 2020. While, there were many more events that took place, I believe that these 4 were the most important ones. The negative effects of these events outweighs the positive ones, making this year become quite worrisome. Let's hope that from April, everything gets back to normal, and the world becomes a free place again. Till then, take care, be safe. Thanks for reading!

ePrabhavnomics blog 84
Originally Published on: 12 April 2020

Why the Coronavirus deaths rates are different in every country?

Even after several weeks of this coronavirus pandemic, things don't seem to come under control, in fact in some countries the situation is getting worse. Most countries have seen a larger number of recoveries compared to deaths, while a few have seen a significantly greater number of deaths. This blog will be looking at why some countries are facing a higher death rate compared to others. The blog will compare death rates by looking at the 'number of deaths per 1 million people', (/1M), rather than the sheer number of deaths. Hope you enjoy this blog!

Firstly we have, median age of the population. Median age of the population is the age that divides the population into two equal sized groups. The first group is younger than the median age, and the second group is older than the median age. Countries with a higher median age, tend to have a larger percentage of people who are older than 65 years. And, the coronavirus is more likely to kill older people. The statistics support this claim, because the countries with a higher median age, mostly have a higher death rate. Examples include; Italy, which has a death rate of 322/1M and a median age of 46.5 years. Spain also, has a high death rate of 355/1M and a median age of 43.9 years. An exception to this rule is Japan, whose median age is higher than Spain and Italy (48.6 years), but has a really low death rate (0.9/1M).

Next we have, age and severity of symptoms in tested patients. What this means is, the average age of tested patients, and the symptoms faced by tested patients (mild/critical). In Italy, the people who were young and/or had mild symptoms weren't tested. Due to this, they wouldn't have taken the precautionary measures, and passed the virus to more vulnerable people. Germany has tested a larger percentage of the young population, and more people with mild symptoms, which allowed them to take the precautionary measures. As a result of this, Germany has a low death rate of 34/1M.

Next is; number of cases at lockdown. The countries which started the lockdown early (at fewer cases) are more likely to contain the virus's spread, which reduces chances of having high death rates. While Italy was one of the first countries to start a complete lockdown (9 March), it already had 9172 cases (at start of lockdown). Similarly, the US, started its lockdown (19-24 March, state by state), when it between 13,865 cases (19 March) to 55,222 (24 March), and is now the country with most cases, and a death rate of 62/1M, the 15th highest in the world. India on the other hand only had 657 cases at the start of its lockdown (25 March), and has one of the lowest death rates, 0.2/1M.

Lastly we have, the health care facility in the country. This includes, number of hospital beds in the ICU (intensive care unit) and ventilators available. Countries with low number of beds per 100,000 people, like Spain (10/100,000) and Italy (12/100,000) had high deaths rates. Germany on the other hand had 29 beds per 100,000 people. There were some exceptions however, for example, US had 34 beds per 100,000, and a high death rate. Meanwhile, South Korea which only had 10.6 beds per 100,000 people had a low death rate of 4/1M.

In conclusion, these were the 4 factors which influenced a country's death rate. In my opinion, all four factors had equal importance in affecting a country's death rate, which is why development of a country and death rate aren't directly proportional. Some factors weren't really in the country's control, like median age and health care facility. However, the virus could have been contained if the other two factors were properly taken into account. Let's hope that the coronavirus spread slows down in the coming weeks. Till then stay safe! And hope you enjoyed this blog! Thanks for reading!

ePrabhavnomics blog 85
Originally Published on: 19 April 2020

Which countries' economy will be most affected by this pandemic?

The ongoing coronavirus pandemic which has put most countries in quarantine, will definitely lead to the countries' economies being affected, with a drop in the countries' total output. I have already written a blog on the negative effects of an epidemic, a the spread of a disease across a nation (blog 76), and a pandemic, the spread of a disease worldwide (blog 80). However, the extent to which the economy faces a loss, will be different for each country. This blog will be looking at which country are more likely to be affected by the coronavirus pandemic. So hope you like it!

The first point is; the structure of the economy. The structure of the economy tells the percentage of output that comes from each sector of the economy (primary, secondary and tertiary). The primary sector involves agricultural activities, such as farming and fishing. The secondary sectors involves the manufacturing of goods. And finally, the tertiary sector is the sector, where services are provided, like teaching. There is a certain correlation between a country's income level and the structure of its economy. Below is a table, which shows each income level, and a rough contribution to GDP (%) from each sector.

	Primary Sector	Secondary Sector	Tertiary Sector
High Income Country	5%	30%	65%
Middle Income Country	10%	35%	55%
Low Income Country	20%	45%	35%

The workers in the primary and secondary sector need to be present at the workplace, while due to current technology, tertiary sector workers don't need to be at the workplace. From the table it is evident that most of the high income countries' GDP contribution comes from the tertiary sector. While most low income country jobs require the workers to be present at the workplace. So, low income countries will see the biggest economic downfall, while most jobs in high income countries can still continue normal work, so high income countries won't face such a huge loss (but will see a slowdown in economic growth). And, more workers in low income countries will go unemployed, while in high income countries, this won't be the case, as work will continue as normal.

Next is; countries dependent on trade and/or tourism. Both these factors can largely help a country, with exports and tourism, aggregate demand (AD), of the country increases, so more cash is injected in the economy. And with imports a country can get access to the goods it can't produce. This pandemic has restricted international travel, so these dependent countries will find it hard to increase their GDP or the quantity of goods they can't produce. And, it will take several months for travel to re-start, so these countries will have to wait for a long time, before getting their days of 'glory' back.

Lastly we have; size of government budget. The more government budget, the less affected the country will be. The government can use its budget to spend in healthcare, to help the situation get better (quicker). The government can also, use its budget to help the unemployed people, so that they can still purchase their saving in this period.

In conclusion, these were the 3 factors which can decide which country will be most affected by this pandemic. The importance of each of these factors is somewhat equal, because even if a country falls in one of these categories, their economy can be severely affected.

Hope you liked this blog! Thanks for reading! Stay safe!

ePrabhavnomics blog 86

Originally Published on: 26 April 2020

What can be done to help the economy after lockdown ends?

After many months of lockdown, many countries are deciding to ease their lockdown restrictions. One of the major impacts this pandemic has had on the world was, a decline in the global economy. After the quarantine ends, the world will have to start working together to help rejuvenate the world economy, since a decline in the global economy can also affect us. This blog will be looking at what can be done to help revive the global economy. So, hope you like this blog! Before starting I would like to note that, due to fear among people (which can remain for a long time), the world economy won't recover soon, so it is better if we don't expect to see progress immediately. However, we all can still try our best to achieve the goal of helping revive the world economy.

The first thing is, the government can give incentives to industries in the primary and secondary sector (those were workers have to be physically present in the workplace), so that they will be able to restart with their production, and achieve a large quantity of output produced, even with fewer people at the workplace. Incentives which the government can provide include: raw material and financial aid. The industries can do two-shifts, one in the morning and one in the afternoon, for a while. Due to this, the chances of the virus getting transmitted among workers reduces. While this might help the industry's production increase rapidly, the employees might have low pay for a while, since the firms will have to invest more in production. But, as demand for the good rises, workers can get their normal pay again.

Apart from just giving them incentives, the government needs to help them by giving them some guidelines to follow. Examples of them include; number of workers allowed in a shift and if there will be different requirements on how to operate the firm. This can help the industries become aware of them, and help them settle down in adherence to these new rules. The quicker they get used to the new guidelines, the faster they can restart production and, the quicker it will start its benefit on the economy.

The next thing is, continue with the coronavirus safety precautions for a few months to a year. Coronavirus safety precautions include, wash your hands regularly, avoid social gatherings and stay home when unwell. The reason for this is, if you are able to avoid getting the virus transmitted or catching the virus, it will not only benefit you and other people, but it can also help avoid a potential second lockdown, which would be bad news for the economy, again. It would also help many industries, since there would be fewer absences when people are in good health. The fewer absences can help the company not see a fall in production.

Lastly, once lockdown ends, you can help the primary and secondary sector industries (read blog 85 to know more on them), by buying more of their goods. Since these industries were most affected by the lockdown, they are also the ones who are in need of most profit. By purchasing their goods, you help the firms get more revenue, which they can later use to produce more goods. This will help many people including, the individual workers, the firms as a whole and the economy. This point isn't forcing anyone to buy products they don't want, but it is encouraging people to possibly spend more on goods coming from the primary and secondary sectors.

In conclusion, these were few things we could do to help revive the economy after the lockdown is over. This was based on my opinion, and it is possible that different countries might use different steps to rejuvenate their economy. Let's see what each country does after they end their lockdown, and if their plans were successful in helping their economy. Hope you liked this blog! Thanks for reading! Be patient, as lockdown is almost going to end!

ePrabhavnomics blog 87
Originally Published on: 3 May 2020

Europe's plans to reopen its tourism industry

One of the major effects of this coronavirus pandemic was: a drop in tourism. After this lockdown, not only has air travel been restricted, but also most individuals are not willing to travel, due to fear. This fear will remain even after the lockdown is over in every country, and the number of active cases (worldwide) drops to zero. This means that, tourism will remain stagnant for a while. Tourism is important for every country's economy, as it gives employment to some people and helps the economy generate revenue. This blog will be looking at Europe's plan to reopen its tourism industry, and how effective I think the plan will be. So, hope you like this blog!

First of all, some European countries are planning to create 'tourist corridors', in which people will still have to practice social distancing, and there will still be testing programmes, so that the spread of the virus can be controlled. Examples of countries which have agreed to this plan include: Czech Republic, which is considering creating a tourist corridor with Slovakia and Croatia. These 3 countries were some of the least infected countries. Countries like: Spain, Italy and the UK (some of the most infected countries) won't be included in the early trials of such a plan. I believe this is a good initiative, so that people can enjoy their summer holidays, while containing themselves from catching the virus. However, it also depends if many people are comfortable with practicing social distancing or not.

The members of the EU will have to follow some guidelines for opening resorts and beaches, which definitely includes social distancing, and prevents the beaches from being overcrowded. One Italian company also started constructing 'plexiglass beach boxes', they are transparent wards, with a height of 2 metres, and width of 4.5 metres. This will allow families to maintain social distancing at the beach. While the again, helps people avoid catching the virus when on holiday, it seems doubtful that people will want to come to the beach, when required to maintain social distancing. This is mainly because, it will be hard for the people to move around the beach (something which many people do regularly when at the beach), which will lead to their enjoyment being restricted. So in conclusion, according to me this plan won't be very successful in attracting tourists to the beach.

Greece's tourism minister has mentioned 'specific new rules' for tourists this summer. Greece is a country that relies heavily on tourism, since 20% of its GDP (around US$40 billion) comes from tourism, for this reason Greece is forced to reopen tourism in the country. While the rules haven't been finalised, the tourism minister of Greece spoken about there being new rules for: hotels, beaches, pools, breakfast buffets and tour buses. He even mentioned possible temperature checks and blood tests when passengers landed in the country. It is hard to comment on their effectiveness now, and will wait till when they are announced. I however also believe that, the checks need to be regularly, not only at time of arrival, or else the virus spread can't be contained.

Some countries, like Germany, haven't agreed to this plan, and has warned other EU to not allow tourists too soon. Germany believes that allowing tourists too early could lead to more virus outbreaks. While other countries are easing their lockdown restrictions, Germany on the other hand is preparing itself for a second wave of coronavirus. Germany is also building more beds, and trying to increase its intensive care capacity. This is a great initiative because, we still don't know if the virus will end this soon or not, so avoiding international travel seems like a better option.

In conclusion, these were few of the plans made by different European countries to reopen their tourism industry, for the summer. While these initiatives are good, it depends on fear amongst people, and how comfortable they are with social distancing. The world will still have to wait for quite a long time before number of international tourists rises to the same level as it was before the lockdown. Anyways hope you liked this blog! Thanks for reading!

ePrabhavnomics blog 88

Originally Published on: 10 May 2020

Economic effects of closing the wet markets post lockdown

The current worldwide pandemic (the coronavirus) and the 2002 SARS (severe acute respiratory syndrome) outbreak, are believed to have originated from the same place, which is: the wet market (in China). For those who don't know, the wet markets are markets where fresh meat (including many animals) and many perishable goods are sold, this is different from the dry market, where they sell clothes and electronics. After this pandemic, many countries have requested China to close its wet markets. This blog will be looking at the effects closing the wet market will have on the economy. So, hope you like this blog! PS: Many countries have wet markets, but this blog will only focus on those in China, since they are the most popular worldwide, and were the inception of both virus outbreaks.

The closure of the wet markets could avert any future pandemics, and preserve most of the wildlife animals. This doesn't mean that all disease outbreaks have originated in the wet market, but it means that, the wet market is responsible for 2 virus outbreaks, and possible risks of virus outbreaks can be prevented in the future. A pandemic has many negative effects on the economy (blog 80 talks about all of them). And secondly, wildlife can be preserved. Most of the Chinese wet markets sell different animals, like bats, which many the population eats. The closure of the wet markets can help these animals, since it will stop people from selling them.

The economy will definitely see a decline. The wet markets have comprised a large percentage of China's economy (exact percentage unknown). Shutting them down will obviously lead to a fall in the economy, since fewer goods will be sold. The country has already faced an economic decline due to the lockdown, after many years of fast economic growth (from over 6% every year to now -7%), so recovering might become harder for the country. However, this (the closure) can help increase demand for other and maybe healthier types of foods in the country, which will help the country's total GDP grow (due to growing demand). The amount of time it takes the economy to start growing fast depends on how fast the Chinese people are able to change and adapt to new food habits. So in conclusion, though the economy will still see a decline after the lockdown ends and the wet markets are closed, it could start growing faster.

Empowering Chinese farmers. Without the wet markets, the farmers (who were one of the most affected by the lockdown) will be have the opportunity to supply more of their agricultural foods to the Chinese population, which will get them more profits. Still, 26% of China's total employees are employed in agriculture, so a huge portion of China's population will be benefitted by closed wet markets. It is true that, it isn't easy to increase supply of agricultural goods, since there isn't unlimited land, the farmers can get more limelight, and earn more. The extra earning can be used to invest in better technology, which has helped increase China's agricultural production over the years. However, this majorly depends on what the Chinese population's taste changes to, if more agricultural goods are demanded, then the farmers will definitely benefit.

In conclusion, these were the few effects which closing wet markets will have on the Chinese economy, it will take some time for those effects of show, since it requires a huge population (1.4 billion) to change their eating habits. But, the result is always positive. If the wet markets are to stay open, since many Chinese prefer the wet market due to, them being cheaper and the availability of 'fresh' food there, the sense of hygiene (at the wet markets) should be improved. Since, with better hygiene the chances of transmitting these diseases (animal to human) drops.

Hope you liked this blog! Thanks for reading! What are your views on the wet market? Should they be closed?

ePrabhavnomics blog 89
Originally Published on: 17 May 2020

Europe's plan to end lockdown

So as you may know, lockdown in many countries is coming to an end. Even if the lockdown isn't completely over, the public restrictions have been eased, and travelling around is possible. Many countries in Europe are planning to reopen different places in the country one-by-one, rather than altogether. This blog will be looking at the plans of few selected countries in more detail, and looking at the economic impacts of this decision. So hope you like this blog!

Let's start by looking at Germany. While Germany is ranked 8th in the world when it comes to total cases, and 6th in Europe. It has managed to keep a low death rate of 96 deaths per 1 million people, and Germany's active cases (number of infected people) reached its peak on 6 April, and has been declining ever since. Germany started by reopening the 'small' shops (smaller than 800 square metres) on 20 April, after that on 4 May, playgrounds, museums and churches were allowed to reopen, later even hair salons opened. And on 11 May many schools (with social distancing rules) reopened. There are still few places which remain closed like bars, restaurants, theatres. Since Germany has managed to control the spread of the virus, reasonably well, it is good that these businesses can reopen (with certain rules). Due to this these businesses can benefit and so can the economy.

Next, let's look at Italy. While it took much longer for Italy to reach its peak of active cases (on 20 April), and was one of the most affected countries, with a significant rise in total cases, total deaths and active cases, Italy is now showing progress, with active cases falling everyday, and total cases rising more slowly (despite 2 weeks after end of lockdown). On 4 May Italy ended its lockdown with more relaxed measures, and is due to open: bars, restaurants, hairdressers on 1 June. One 18 May, shops, museums and libraries will open. Seeing how Italy is now managing to keep the cases under control (to some extent), this seems like a good plan, which can possibly benefit many firms, and the economy.

Moving onto Russia. Russia has the 2nd highest number of total cases in the world (behind USA). Russia is still seeing a steep increase in daily new cases and active cases are still rising, though the death rate is very low (18 deaths per 1 million people). Moscow (the worst-hit city) is keeping restrictions till 31 May (could extend), while other places relaxed the restrictions on 12 May. People were forced to put gloves and masks in shops and on public transport, and only food shops and pharmacies were allowed to open, along with construction sites. It is tempting to reopen these sites, to reduce unemployment rates and stop the economy from shrinking, but for Russia it is better to stay in total lockdown, until cases come under control.

Lastly I will talk about France. France is also a country badly infected by the coronavirus. France still has a high death rate (423 deaths per 1 million people), which is still lower than that of many badly affected countries. France over the past few weeks has seen a drop in active cases and daily new cases. France has allowed shops and leisure centres to reopen, but bars and restaurants will stay closed. The gatherings must be restricted to only 10 people. Beaches have started to reopen as well. It is best if France keeps these restrictions for a little longer, and only reopens when active cases are very low.

Overall, this is what 4 European countries are doing to end their lockdown, and what I feel about their plans. Their plans will most probably change depending on what happens to the number of cases in the countries. On the side note, all these countries are planning to open their borders between early to mid June, to allow international tourists (only from Europe). I have already written a blog on Europe's plan to reopen tourism and its impacts (blog 87), and I feel that it is still to early to open international borders.

Anyways, hope you liked this blog! Thanks for reading! Next week I will be looking at other European countries' plans.

ePrabhavnomics blog 90
Originally Published on: 24 May 2020

Europe's plan to end lockdown (2)

Last week I wrote a blog on what some European countries are doing to end their lockdown. At the end of that blog I promised that this week, I will be writing about more European countries' plans to reopen the country, and looking at the economic effects of this plan. I will also be judging if these decisions are good, based on the death rates and total number of active coronavirus cases (currently infected), and their trend (increasing or decreasing). So hope you like this blog!

We will start by looking at Belgium. When it comes to total cases (both active and closed), Belgium ranks 18th in the world.

However, Belgium has one of the highest death rates with 797 deaths per 1 million people. While the rise in total cases and total deaths is slowing down, the number of active cases are still rising (though slowly). Belgium formally ended its lockdown on 4 May, and since 10 May households were allowed to host maximum 4 guests. Shops opened on 11 May, with people forced to follow social distancing rules and schools reopened on 18 May, with a maximum of 10 children allowed in every classroom. Apart from that, many markets, museums, zoos, hairdressers are reopened on 18 May. Restaurants are expected to open on 8 June. In my opinion, while it is true that Belgium's economy is declining (by a huge amount, around -3%), it is best to extend the lockdown, since active cases are still rising, and there is a higher chance of dying in Belgium (high death rate). Even if it will cost the economy even more, it is better to save lives.

Next we will look at Netherlands. Netherlands is ranked 20th in the world when it comes to total cases. Netherlands is seeing a drop in the rise in total cases and total deaths. Netherlands is ranked 10th in terms of death rates (339 per 1 million people). On 11 May, they started by reopening libraries, hairdressers and nail bars. Bars and restaurants are due to open from 1 June, with a maximum of 30 guests inside, and people will have to keep a distance of 1.5m between each other. Theatres, will also open on 1 June, with the same rules are restaurants. Campsites and holiday parks are due to reopen on 1 July, and restaurants and theatres can allow uptown 100 people (with social distancing). Schools are going to reopen on 2 June. This is a good initiative, since the country isn't reopening in a short span of time (unlike Belgium), due to this, the number of people leaving their houses won't be too high, and the country can contain the spread, and it will help the economy regrow. However, people still need to be careful, since the death rate is quite high.

Next is Denmark. Denmark isn't as badly hit as many other countries in Europe. Its death rate is quite low (97 deaths per 1 million people). The daily rise in total deaths and total cases is minimal in the country, and active cases are falling steeply. The lockdown restrictions were eased starting from mid-April, with primary school children returning to school on 14 April (secondary school children on 18 May). Hairdressers and beauty salons reopened on 20 April, and shopping centres on 11 May (with social distancing guidelines). Restaurants and theatres opened on 18 May and 21 May respectively. In early August, gyms, pools and nightclubs are expected to reopen. This is definitely, a great plan, since the country is able to contain the virus spread, and reopening will help the economy regrow. Not reopening everything in a short time span will help limit the number of people outside.

Lastly, we will talk about Spain. Spain is one of the worst hit countries, it is ranked 4th when it comes to total cases, and has a high death rate (613 deaths per 1 million people). Spain is still seeing a huge rise in total cases (daily), and while active cases are generally seeing a downward trend, it isn't consistent. From 21 May, wearing masks is obligatory, even inside, if social distance isn't possible. Schools are going to be partially reopened on 26 May, along with cinemas, theatres. Cinemas will only have a 30% capacity, and concerts will only allow 400 people (with social distancing). From 10 June, restaurants will reopen with social distancing rules placed. I believe that, Spain should wait for few weeks more, before starting the reopening, due to high deaths rates, and still rapidly rising cases. This will cost many people and the economy, but saving lives is more important.

Overall, these were the plans of 4 more European countries in restarting life after lockdown. And if in my opinion, these plans look good or not, depending on the current coronavirus situation in the country, and also analysing the economic effects of the plan. Hope you liked this blog! Thanks for reading!

ePrabhavnomics blog 91
Originally Published on: 31 May 2020

India's lockdown and plan to reopen the country

In many parts of the world the coronavirus pandemic is showing no signs of stopping, with the total cases in the world having crossed 6 million, and many countries still seeing steep increases in total cases. One such country, which is still experiencing rapid increases in total coronavirus cases is India. India has reached the 7th spot (in the world) in terms of total cases, and is showing no progress in containing the virus. However, the government of India has decided to open the country on 31 May, despite this. This blog will be looking at why India is taking such a step, and its possible economic impacts. So, hope you like this blog!

Before starting I would like to give a brief history of the virus in India, and India's lockdown dates. India's first case was recorded on 15 February. Later, on 25 March India started its lockdown (with 657 cases in the country), scheduled to end on 14 April (the number of cases had increased to 11,487 on this day). So lockdown was extended to 3 May (42,505 cases on this day). Later it was extended again to 17 May, (95,698 cases on this day), and is finally going to end today (with restrictions in place). Even after such a long lockdown period the country has seen more than 183,000 confirmed cases.

The lockdown has definitely affected many people in India (like every other country with lockdown). The daily wage (migrant) workers have been severely affected by the lockdown. This is mainly because, their wages are very low and with businesses shut down, they become unemployed and therefore can't afford food or any basic necessity. These workers can't even return home, due to the closing of railway lines. All businesses were shut down, which made them lose lots of revenue. And lastly, India faced a food shortage, since everyone has to stay home, everyone will need to buy more food. And this put lots of pressure on India's food supply, that had to feed 1.4 billion people.

Just recently, the Minister of Home Affairs (MHA) has issued guidelines for the public to follow till 30 June (at least). These guidelines are part of the 'Lockdown 5.0', and are divided in 3 phases. In Phase 1 from 8 June, religious places, shopping malls, hotels, restaurants and other hospitality services will open. In Phase 2, the MHA is planning to open schools (and other educational institutions). However, this decision will be taken in July, only after discussing this with teachers, parents and the institutes (and also with the States). In Phase 3, international travel, cinema halls, parks and other unopened things will reopen, after analysing the situation then. As of now, businesses and construction has restarted.

This plan is similar to that of many countries (especially European ones), in which the country is planning to reopen its services in groups, rather than all together. While I believe India's numbers are still too high for complete lockdown (lockdown with more restrictions) to end, I can understand the government's concerns of the Indian economy seeing a declining. This is a good initiative too help the country's businesses restart again, and help the economy grow again. However, strict action must be taken against those breaking these restrictions, or else the step rise in total cases will never end. I also believe that the Indian government should have given more support to the migrant workers during the lockdown, for example give the more financial aid.

In conclusion, this was my blog on India's lockdown history, who has been most affected by this lockdown, the MHA's plan to reopen the country and my opinion of the plan's economic effects. Let's see how the number of total cases changes in the upcoming days, with the hope that they will see a fall, and let's see if there is a change in plan.

Hope you liked this blog! Thanks for reading!

ePrabhavnomics blog 92
Originally Published on: 7 June 2020

Effects of a natural disaster on the economy

Just recently, the city of Mumbai, India was hit by a deadly cyclone named the 'Cyclone Nisarga'. While the city did see heavy rainfall over the past few days, and some deaths, it fortunately managed to mostly stay safe from facing a great amount of damage. This is fortunate for the city, for many reasons, including the current coronavirus pandemic, which Mumbai is greatly suffering from. This is because the negative effects of the pandemic and the cyclone damage would be huge. This blog will be looking solely at the effects of any natural disaster on the economy. So, hope you like this blog!

Firstly, the government will have to spend lots in helping evacuate the people from that area, before the disaster. While this is not always successful, if there are forecasts of a possible huge disaster, the government might decide to evacuate the population out of the area, so that they don't face injuries or lose their lives. This will cost the government lots of money, for example, the cost of transportation, the cost of living. This is a huge risk for the government, since the plan could become a failure, and people may not co-operate with the plans.

The government has to spend a large amount of money on reparations (regardless of an evacuation). While the exact reparation amount depends on the amount of damage caused, usually the costs of reparation are very high. It is possible that (especially for poorer countries) the government might not have enough money to pay for these damages. While the country facing the natural disaster can call other countries for help (which the other countries normally respond too and help), it is always easier to have the appropriate infrastructure and resources to either prevent huge damage, or take care of the damage themselves. And plus, there is no certainty on how long it will take the damages to be fixed. The government is most likely to buy reparation resources from foreign countries, so the government spending (which is a component of aggregate demand) won't really help the local economy.

All the following points are assuming no evacuation has taken place.

Natural disasters will also affect the health of individuals in the economy. The damage can easily contaminate the food and water in the economy. For example, during the 2011 Earthquake and Tsunami in Japan. The Fukushima nuclear power plant was damaged, and this made radiation appear in local milk and vegetables. It is possible that many people in the affected area are unaware of this, and consume the contaminated food. This doesn't only affected the individuals, but also the hospitals, since the hospitals will already be having to look after many patients who are facing injuries due to the damage. The government will have to spend more on the country's health care, and spend less on reparations. Which will possibly mean that it will take more time for the reparation work to end.

It can lead to a rise in prices of food and oil, amongst other necessities. Due to natural disasters there can easily be a reduction in the quantity of basic necessities, like oil, especially since the factories producing these goods are very likely to be destroyed. The government will have to raise their prices, to control the excess demand for now even more limited quantity. This affects the population, since the disaster has possibly (already) made the public lose their jobs, and now they will have to face higher costs when buying their necessities. And this will lead to an overall decline in quality of life in the affected area.

And lastly, as mentioned in the last point, businesses and workers will face a loss. Many businesses are prone to getting severely damaged due to natural disasters, which suspends any production from taking place. Since the businesses are closed, workers also face unemployment. Since, the size of the damage and how long it will take to repair the damage is different for every incident, we can't tell how long the unemployment will prevail. However, it is clear that the more the damage the longer people will be unemployed for, and the more it will affect the economy.

So, this was my blog on the economic effects of a natural disaster. As you can see from the blog, there are no positive effects, therefore it is always better if the country has the sufficient infrastructure to prevent huge damage, and the public is aware of what they can do to help save their lives. However, unfortunately this is not the case for every country, but hopefully as time passes these countries will have this strong infrastructure as well.

Hope you liked this blog! Thanks for reading!

ePrabhavnomics blog 93
Originally Published on: 14 June 2020

The economic effects of the George Floyd protests

Since 26 May, the United States of America has had the 'George Floyd protests' going on, in which the public is protesting against racism and police brutality. These protests started due to a dark skinned man, 'George Floyd', being mercilessly killed by a fair skinned police officer. After the US, people in many countries have started these protests as well. The US has already seen a decline in the economy due to the COVID-19 pandemic, which forced many businesses to shut down, and now these protests will lead to even worse effects for the US economy. This blog will look at how these protests will affect the US economy. So, hope you like this blog!

One of the most affected cities was New York (NYC). During these protests an estimated 450 businesses in NYC were looted or damaged, and is expected to cost these businesses tens of millions of dollars. There were many other cities in the US, apart from NYC which experienced such looting like Minneapolis (the epicentre of these protests). The total value of the items looted in Minneapolis (alone) is an estimated $350,000. Businesses will definitely face lots of difficulty in recovering and restarting. The coronavirus pandemic is also responsible for the businesses' increased difficulty, since many businesses weren't seeing any revenue gain in the past few months. The longer it takes the business to recover, the longer the economy will suffer, as during that period, the economy won't see any production. And due to this, the population won't be able to purchase the goods they need.

The next point is, lack of employment. Since these protests have destroyed many businesses, the population is also left jobless. Until the businesses don't restart the population will be out of work, and it is unknown when these businesses will see light of day again. Again, due to the coronavirus pandemic these people were already unemployed, and sadly, their troubles will continue for longer. This will not only affect them, but also the economy, since the government will be forced to provide them with aid, (fun fact: just few days ago 1.5 million US workers applied for unemployment benefits), while simultaneously helping to restart businesses.

The property owners and insurance companies will also be faced with huge costs. During these protests not only businesses, but even many buildings have been burnt. The owners that are insured, won't have to face this cost of since the insurance company will give them this compensation. However, owners without insurance are in trouble, and will have to unfortunately find a solution themselves. Meanwhile, insurance companies will have to provide compensation to the owners with damaged buildings. While property owners will be in more trouble than insurance companies (since it is very unlikely insurance companies go broke), both of them will still have to spend a large amount of their money. This will affect the economy, since it is unclear when and how the uninsured property will manage to get is compensation, and resume functioning as before. And, if in the unlikely event, insurance companies go broke, the property owners will have more difficulty in recovering.

Lastly, the deaths and injuries of many people. There have been many deaths and injuries across the country during these protests. While the deaths and injuries of people is always something unfortunate, it is worse to get an injury in this situation. This is because even now the US is booming when it comes to coronavirus cases, due to which the hospitals are running at full capacity, it will be harder to find space in hospitals to get treatment. This will mean that, the government will again have to focus on investing in the country's health care system. The government overall will have to face the burden of investing in many areas of the country.

In conclusion, from this blog we can see that the whole country is getting affected due to these protests; the government, businesses, employees, property owners and insurance companies. The coronavirus pandemic has contributed in making the economic situation in the country worse.

Anyways, hope you liked this blog! Thanks for reading! Let's hope these protests end soon, and justice is delivered!

ePrabhavnomics blog 94
Originally Published on: 21 June 2020

Effects of yoga on the economy

Today (21 June) is International Yoga Day 2020. Yoga in simple language is defined as 'a spiritual and ascetic discipline, which includes breath control, meditation and the adoption of different bodily postures'. Yoga originated in India thousands of years ago, and over the years has managed to gain popularity in many countries, and is now practised worldwide. If more people practise yoga, it can benefit the economy. This blog will discuss the effects of yoga on the economy. So, hope you like this blog.

Firstly, yoga can improve your physical and mental health. Physical benefits include; better athletic performance, weight reduction, better cardio and circulatory health, improves body flexibility. And mental health benefits include, lower stress levels, increased concentration. Improved physical health, benefits an individual in many ways, such as, lower chances of catching diseases, or getting sick. This benefits the economy, because this means, fewer absences from work. When the percentage attendance at work increases, the productivity of that company most likely increases. If we add the extra output made by every company, we see there is a huge increased output in the economy.

Relating to the previous point, in the current situation when the world is facing a global pandemic, the coronavirus, doing yoga can reduce your chances of getting the virus. Again, because yoga improves your bodily health. There are many negative impacts which this pandemic has had on the economy, such as unemployment, businesses face a loss in revenue, (explained in more detail in blog 80), and if lesser people are infected by the virus, the better it is for the global economy. This doesn't mean doing yoga will avoid a global pandemic, but it can help to reduce the number of people getting infected, or can help speed up recovery. This will mean that the period of lockdown will be short, and can help the global economy not face a huge loss.

Improved mental health can help overall in being more happier in life. As mentioned earlier, improved mental health can lower stress levels in life, and can increase brain concentration among many other things, including: clearer thinking, more self-esteem, lower chances of depression. All of these factors can help an individual focus more on his and work and feel better and confident about them-self. With more and better focus on your work, you can improve your productivity and efficiency (do more work in less time), this will not only benefit the economy, but giving it more output, but can also help the individuals, as they can get a salary increase.

And lastly, doing yoga can help the yoga industry grow. Currently yoga is practised by 300 million people worldwide, and the number is expected to grow over the years. The total value of the yoga industry worldwide is $84 billion. This industry is already the fastest growing industry in the world, and rightly so. If this industry grows, it will not only help more people in the world, but will allow the industry to improve itself, which can help people get better facilities for practising. If the industry increases in value, it can help the economy, since the aggregate demand (AD) of the economy (and of the world) will rise, and this will mean more cash is entering the economy.

While yoga can help your body, it can also harm your body. A lot of the negative impacts of yoga occur during the practise, when you try and go beyond your limitations. Possible harms yoga can do to your body include: muscle strain or back injury. While they aren't serious injuries, continuously trying to go beyond your shortcomings isn't something good. Other serious problems yoga can cause to you include, high blood pressure, due to forceful breathing and inversion poses. And also you can have problems with your eyesight, if you give your eyes too much pressure.

So, this was my blog on how yoga affects the economy. As you can see most of the effects are positive, and as I have told the negative effects as well hopefully you will be able to avoid them. Anyways, Happy Yoga Day. Hope you liked this blog! Thanks for reading!

ePrabhavnomics blog 95
Originally Published on: 28 June 2020

Economic effects of boycotting Chinese products

The world is facing a global pandemic, the coronavirus, for several months. It is believed that the coronavirus started in China's wet markets, mainly due to Chinese people's poor eating habits. After this incident, many countries have started campaigns to boycott Chinese products. Countries wanting to enforce this boycott include, Australia, India, Philippines, US, UK, Vietnam and Tibet. So, in this blog I will be explaining the economic effects of boycotting Chinese products. So hope you like this blog!

Before starting I would like to state that a complete boycott of Chinese products is very hard, and will definitely take lots of time. This is because, China exports billion dollars worth of goods annually. For example, every year US$671 billion of 'Electrical machinery equipment' is exported by China. Other highly exported goods include: plastics & plastic articles ($84.4 billion), vehicles ($74.4 billion) & medical apparatus ($73 billion), among other goods. This shows that Chinese goods have a very high demand worldwide, and being able to boycott these goods immediately won't be possible. However, there are still many advantages of this boycott.

The first advantage is that, countries can reduce their overall spending on imports. Due to this, the balance of payments (BoP), which is the difference between cash inflows and cash outflows can see a surplus. One of the main cash inflows is cash received from exports, and one of the main cash outflows is the cash payed to buy imports. If these countries decide to not buy Chinese goods, there BoP will see a greater surplus (assuming trade figures with other countries remains the same). There are many disadvantages for a country that has a BoP deficit (blog 42 explains them), so therefore the country can avoid many potential disadvantages if they have a BoP surplus.

Boycotting Chinese products can help countries become more independent. When countries heavily import from another country, they highly depend on that foreign country and it is highly unlikely that they produce mass amounts of that good. When a country decides to boycott a foreign country's goods, from whom they having been purchasing large quantities of goods (reference to paragraph 2), they are indirectly also planning to become more independent. This is because, they are unsure if they will find another alternative (country) from where they can buy that same good, therefore they have to themselves plan to produce that good, in large quantities. If a country is successful at producing the goods they boycotted, it can even help them see a growth in their economy, since overall output produced rises. The BoP surplus they will potentially have, by spending less on imports, can be used to help the country produce the good(s) they boycotted.

There are still some disadvantages of this boycott. For example, higher taxes for consumers. Since the country wants to produce more goods, the consumers might be taxed more, so that the government can give more financial aid to the firms. While the higher BoP surplus could be used to produce the extra goods, it is uncertain if that money is already going to be used somewhere else. Higher taxes will affect consumers at any time, but in the current scenario, when the economy has seen a downfall, due to the coronavirus pandemic, taking this step will hurt the consumers quite badly.

Overall, this was my blog on how boycotting Chinese products will affect the countries taking up this boycott. It can be seen that this boycott gives the country more advantages (along with opportunities), when compared to disadvantages. However, the boycott shouldn't be done immediately, it should be carefully planned out, and only then executed. Anyways, hope you liked this blog! Thanks for reading!

ePrabhavnomics blog 96
Originally Published on: 5 July 2020

Economic impacts of the China-India skirmishes

Since the 5th of May, there has been a skirmish going on between India and China. The skirmish is being fought along the Sino-Indian border, in places including: the disputed Pangong Lake (in Ladakh), the Tibet Autonomous Region (TAR), near the border of Sikkim and in much of Eastern Ladakh along the 'Line of Actual Control (LAC). There are different reasons for this dispute taking place, one of them involving, both countries fighting for getting full control of the LAC. It has been since 1962 that these countries are fighting for the LAC. This blog will be looking at the economic impacts (in general) of this skirmish. So hope you like this blog!

The ban of China related stuff in India has to some extent already started after this skirmish. Just recently, India banned 59 Chinese apps in the country, including the very popular Tik Tok. The Indian Union Minister for Road Transport and Highways, Nitin Gadkari, also prohibited Chinese companies from taking part in any road projects. The government is also examining the amount of investment made by Chinese in many sectors. This is a good initiative by India to try and become more self-reliant. However, for the moment it is not a good idea for India to completely boycott China. This is because around 12% of India's total imports are from China, however only 3% of India's total exports are to China. This shows that, India needs Chinese exports more than vice-versa. So, for the moment India isn't ready to stop buying Chinese goods. India should work on producing the goods they buy from China. Producing more goods will also help boost India's economy.

India will lose out on Chinese investments. The foreign direct investment (FDI) by China in India was around $1.8 billion between 2015 and 2019, and is overall an important investment source for India. Investment isn't only about money, it is also about technology, knowledge transfer, skills, etc. This investment can potentially help Indian companies become more efficient. While India might be aiming to become more self-reliant, it is better if the country doesn't ignore any help from other countries in improving their infrastructure. And to add to that, India's FDI rules are strong enough to avoid foreigners from creating a monopoly.

China is likely to face trade losses (though minor) if India decides to stop trading with them. Since China exports more to India, it has an overall trade surplus. This is the 4th highest trade surplus China has (after US, Hong Kong and the EU). China's trade surplus from India is $52 billion, while the top 3 countries give China a trade surplus of over $100 billion (US gives it almost $300 billion surplus). For this reason, India's move to boycott Chinese goods may not affect China that much (assuming China's trade balance with other countries remains equal).

Since both the countries are currently facing an economic decline, due to the coronavirus pandemic, it is better if neither of them makes a trade policy, immediately. It is better if both countries negotiate a fair trade policy for the moment, as any hasty decision by any of the two countries could backfire. A trade war between India and China might affect other Asian countries as well, with the countries being forced to choose a side, and this will lead to a huge mess. Therefore, it is better avoiding a trade war, though the trade relationship between the two countries is likely to deteriorate in the future.

So, in conclusion it is apparent that India is more likely to face greater losses, when compared to China. However, India could avoid these losses if the country works on boosting its economy, and producing goods which it imports the most (though it will be hard). Let's hope this skirmish ends soon, and a viable agreement is formed between the two countries. Anyways, hope you liked this blog! Thanks for reading!

ePrabhavnomics blog 97
Originally Published on: 12 July 2020

Future of Airbnb after the pandemic and its effects on the economy

Airbnb is a online marketplace company, based in San Francisco, California. Airbnb's main purpose is to offer housing for tourists. While the company doesn't own any property, it acts like the broker and gets the pay from each booking. The coronavirus has affected Airbnb negatively, with many places wanting to ban it. This blog will be looking at why these places are planning to ban Airbnb, and what effects the ban will have on those economies. So, hope you like this blog!

Starting with the negatives economic effects of banning Airbnb includes: possibly less tourism in the future. Airbnb is one of the many options for tourists, with this option taken away, it is possible that fewer tourists will visit the area in the future. The demand for Airbnb is increasing over the years, with more people renting houses via Airbnb. Therefore the ban will affect a large majority of people who will have to find another alternative when going on holiday. Since, the options aren't unlimited, it could potentially reduce tourist arrivals in these places. Also, Airbnb is cheaper than hotels (alternative), so this dearer price will also prevent tourists from coming. This will negatively impact the economies, since tourism helps the country earn more revenue. However, I also believe that many countries will have started getting used to lower tourism, due to the pandemic people might not resume travelling for a certain period of time.

Another negative effect is: individuals hosting tourists will earn less. People who own many houses can choose which ones to list on Airbnb (which people can later rent). This is a strategy for them to earn more money. However, when many places are planning to get rid of Airbnb, it is a loss for them, since they won't be able to earn the extra money they potentially could have. This might not personally affect them (since they are already quite rich), but it will affect the economy, since the possible spending in the economy won't increase drastically. And therefore, the economy won't see a huge rise in cash inflows.

The first positive effect of this is: more affordable housing for these essential workers. One of the main reasons many places want to get rid of Airbnb is; high rent. This pandemic has already led to many key workers losing their jobs, and it is not ideal for them to have to pay high rent. Banning Airbnb therefore becomes a good initiative (Lisbon is a prime example of a place doing this) in helping to empower these workers, especially since Airbnb's rent has risen over the past. More than the economy, this is a big benefit for these workers, who will in the future find basic goods more affordable (due to spending less on rent).

The next positive effect is: safety of people isn't compromised. As stated previously, many people are unsure about how safe Airbnb is, therefore are unsure of booking by Airbnb. This doesn't mean that Airbnb is definitely unsafe, but it is still possible that the home owners might not be sure of how much sanitising needs to be done, and they might under-do it. This obviously puts at risk the safety of the people renting the Airbnb houses. It is possible that the people renting the houses might be unaware of this, and might catch the virus. It is always better if fewer people catch the virus, not only for the individuals, but also for the economy as a whole. This is because, if fewer people catch the virus, the lesser time it will take for the country to reopen, which can help the economy restart.

Overall, from this blog it is evident that this initiative of getting rid of Airbnb has equal number of benefits and negative effects on the economies. Therefore, it is fair to conclude that this move isn't too good. While it can help improve safety and allow workers to face lower rent, it will leave tourists with dearer alternatives. But, since tourism is halted after this virus, it shouldn't be a huge concern for them, for the time being. So, we can overall say that the negative effects won't heavily impact the people in question. Therefore this initiative is more beneficial. Anyways, hope you liked this blog! Thanks for reading!

ePrabhavnomics blog 98
Originally Published on: 19 July 2020

Impacts of COVID-19 on Higher Education Institutes

The coronavirus pandemic is showing little signs of stopping, with many countries still seeing huge increases (daily) in number of cases. This pandemic has affected many things, like: the economy, many businesses, institutes, and the population. The 'higher education institutes', which consists of Universities and Colleges, is one of the types of institutes facing the biggest losses from this pandemic. This blog will be looking at how the coronavirus will affect Universities and Colleges. So, hope you like this blog!

The first negative effect universities will face is: loss of revenue. This pandemic has created fear in the minds of many people, and it is very likely that they will halt international travel for many years. This will be a loss for universities, since they won't be able to gain revenue from international students. This will affect the universities, since they will have many problems, such as trouble in investing in many different facilities. This could possibly impact the quality of education received by the students. Also, professors in the universities will receive lower income, which will mean they will have difficulty in purchasing their necessities.

In order to avoid a huge loss in revenue, it is possible that the universities hike their fees. Doing this, the universities can earn more from the fewer students that will come. This move will affect both the universities and the students. If students have applied in many universities (locally), they will obviously choose the cheapest option. So, if universities hike their prices too much, many students might back out of them, and it will obviously be a bigger loss for the universities. Meanwhile students that don't have many offers will have to forcefully pay these high fees. Some families might find this fee too expensive to pay, especially because, during the pandemic they had a cut in pay and had to face higher prices when buying basic necessities.

The next negative effect is: possible loss of staff. It is very likely that the universities will be having some international staff, who returned to their hometown before quarantine. It is possible that these staff members might find it difficult to travel back, due to different travel restrictions placed by their country of origin. The University might have to employ new temporary local staff, until the travel restrictions are lifted. There are many problems which the University might face during this process, such as difficulty in finding sufficiently qualified people for the job. And the original staff will be unemployed for longer, which means they will face many difficulties in surviving. However, a solution for this problem is: conduct online lessons. With online lessons, staff members don't need to travel back. But, this solution can only be effective if universities are sufficiently technologically equipped to conduct online lessons, this however is more of a problem for smaller universities.

The University will have to change its setup. Universities will be forced to practice social distancing, and possibly limit the number of students who can be in the university (at any moment in time). It will put some burden on the universities, as they will have to simultaneously plan both lessons and a setup with which the students and staff can conveniently follow social distancing. Again, a solution these universities can adapt to avoid all this hassle is: online lessons. But again, it will depend on how well equipped the University is to conduct these online lessons.

Overall, the coronavirus has affected universities and colleges very negatively, there aren't any real positive benefits of this pandemic on these institutions. However, one thing the University can do to avoid all this is: start online classes. If the university manages to successfully implement this, it can continue teaching lectures and at the same time not have to worry about implementing social distancing rules in the campus, amongst many other problems.

Anyways, hope you liked this blog! Thanks for reading!

ePrabhavnomics blog 99
Originally Published on: 26 July 2020

Progress made by Europe in achieving the SDGs between 2014 and 2019

The Sustainable Development Goals (SDGs) are a set of 17 goals set by the United Nations (UN) in 2015 to act as a 'blueprint to achieve a better and more sustainable future for all'. The UN General Assembly hopes to achieve these goals by 2030. In this blog I will be analysing the progress made by Europe between 2014 and 2019, in the various issues, which the SDGs wish to solve. Achieving these goals can help the economy and also the world can become a better place, I have explained this in blog 13. Hope you like this blog.

The first issue we will be looking at is: gender equality. Goal 5 of SDGs is to achieve 'Gender Equality.' Over the past 5 years,

Europe has unfortunately made regress rather than progress, in achieving this goal, which means the gender gap has widened, though only slightly. The percentage of men of working age employed in 2019, was 11.7 percentage points higher than that of women of the same age range. This figure is 0.1 percentage point higher than 2014. However, when it comes to education, the percentage of women in higher education in 2019, was 10.5 percentage points higher compared to men, and there has been an increasing number of women in senior leadership roles. And people are working on reducing the pay gap. So, overall while Europe might have made some progress in achieving gender equality, Europe has slightly worsened in difference in employment rate between both genders. Which means, women get fewer job opportunities than men. Let's hope Europe sees a positive trend in achieving gender equality, in the next 5 years.

The next issues is: environmental care. Goal 13 is 'Climate Action', and it wishes to fight climate change and its impacts on the world. Here Europe has made some progress. Europe is still working hard to make more progress, such as increasing its use of renewable energy. In 2018, 18.9% of Europe's energy consumed was renewable, and it is working on increasing this percentage to 20% by 2020. The coronavirus lockdown has helped Europe make some progress in improving air quality, because of reduced vehicular traffic for a few months. However, in my opinion this was short lived, since after the lockdown ended, the number of plying on the streets drastically increased again. But still, according to some sources this progress isn't enough, and Europe is 'currently not on-track to meet its 40% emission reduction target by 2030'.

Lastly, I will be looking at: access to justice. Goal 16 is 'Peace, Justice and strong institutions', and this goal wishes to 'end violence, promoting the law, strengthen institutions and increase access to justice'. This is the goal in which Europe has made the most progress, and that too a huge one. The progress done by these countries can be seen due to the fact that, most countries became less corrupt (and 12 of the 20 least corrupt countries are in Europe), expenditure by the general government on law courts has risen, crime rates has fallen in many countries, and more people now have confidence in EU institutions.

If all 17 goals are ranked in order of 'progress made by Europe in achieving them'. 1st place we have Goal 16, which is 'Peace, Justice and strong institutions'. 2nd place we have Goal 1, which is 'No Poverty'. Followed by Goal 3 (Good Health and Well Being), Goal 2 (Zero Hunger), Goal 8 (Decent Work and Economic Growth), Goal 11 (Sustainable Cities and Communities), Goal 4 (Quality Education), Goal 17 (Partnerships for the Goals), Goal 12 (Responsible Consumption and Production), Goal 7 (Affordable and Clean Energy), Goal 10 (Reduced Inequalities), Goal 15 (Life on Land), Goal 9 (Industry, Innovation and Infrastructure), Goal 13 (Climate Action) and lastly Goal 5 (Gender Equality). The goal which hasn't been ranked is Goal 14 (Life Below Water), and this is because it reportedly hard to measure statistics on its progress.

Overall, this was my blog on the progress made by Europe in achieving these 17 SDGs. It is clear from this list, what goals Europe should focus most on in the coming years. But, this change is still positive, especially because there was only one goal in which the situation become worse (Goal 5), otherwise the continent saw an improvement when it came to the other goals. Let's hope these goals are achieved by 2030.

Hope you liked this blog! Thanks for reading!

ePrabhavnomics blog 100
Originally Published on: 2 August 2020

Completion of 100 blogs – History of my blogs

Hello everybody, today I am posting my 100th consecutive blog. So in this blog, rather than looking at a new topic, I go down the memory lane, and present to you a summary of few of my past blogs. Hope you like this blog! And thanks to everyone for supporting me through this journey!

This journey started on 9 September 2018, where I wrote about 'what would happen if 1 Indian rupee equalled 1 US dollar'. This has both positive and negative impacts on India. The positive includes: cheaper to import in India, due to which people can buy more goods and there will be lower transport costs. Meanwhile there were negatives such as: dearer to export from India, loss of jobs due to higher labour costs and lack of investment in India. So, overall this situation, of '1 India rupee equalling 1 US dollar' gives more costs to India, when compared to benefits.

Later, in blog 10 I wrote about 'The economics behind war'. I wrote about how wars can take place due to many different economic reasons like: lack of basic necessities (due to poverty, inequality or unemployment), some countries might want valuable resources which they can't produce, a country might fight to occupy more land or the population is unhappy with the country's leader (the President). 'Scarcity of something' is what is common between these 4 causes of starting a war.

Next in blog 43, I wrote about 'The causes and effects of heatwaves in Europe'. As causes I wrote clear skies (lack of cloud cover), which meant that heat can no longer be absorbed by clouds, therefore causing excess heat. Then, there was warm air coming from North Africa. And lastly, there is climate change taking place in the world, which is a possible reason for the heatwaves. And I explained how it can affect: few groups of people (like sensitive people, children and the elderly), crops (which can't grow) and the infrastructure (melting roads).

In blog 56 I spoke about the 'US-China Trade War and its Impacts'. This trade war will definitely impact both US and China by slowing down their economic growth. And since they are trade partners, this will cause the global economy's growth to decline. However, this trade war can help emerging countries (economies) like Vietnam, who can take this opportunity to increase their trade to both these countries.

Blog 80 was dedicated to the current situation the world is facing, a global pandemic (the coronavirus), and how it would impact the economy. While there were mostly negative impacts like: absences of workers from work, which meant no wages for them and how businesses will lose revenue due to the lockdown. However, there were also positive impacts to this situation like: lower greenhouse gas emissions, due to lower vehicular traffic and it gives people an opportunity to learn new skills.

And in my previous blog (blog 99), I analysed Europe's progress between 2014 & 2019 in achieving the SDGs. In gender equality,

Europe slightly deteriorated, while in peace & justice Europe significantly improved.

So overall, these were the summaries of few of my past blogs. Hope you liked this blog! Thanks for reading! Thanks for your support everyone!

ABOUT THE AUTHOR

The author of this book is an aspiring economist and alumni of the British School of Milan. He believes that the study of Economics is important since it analyses everyday decisions, and their impacts on the society. The author is keen on studying the issues faced by different countries and their causes and effects on the economy. He started sharing his research with his family and friends, which is what inspired him to start writing these blogs. He started publishing them every week on Facebook, and later shifted to WordPress, his blogs became popular on both websites, due to their simple and lucid language, which can be understood even by non-economics students as well as any common man. They were so much appreciated that, some of his friends even used them to revise for their school exams.

Comment by author's teacher:

Prabhav Meharunkar brought to his study of IB Economics at the British School of Milan a very lively interest in real-world events. This enabled him to offer exciting examples in many topics we studied in class, taken from a wide range of countries. In this collection of his blogs, we glimpse Prabhav's enthusiasm, gain insights into his own views as an young economist and are challenged to think more deeply and to be more aware ourselves.

www.ingramcontent.com/pod-product-compliance
Lightning Source LLC
Chambersburg PA
CBHW071555150726
48000CB00004B/1469